The Hackney Crucible

The
Hackney Crucible

MORRIS BECKMAN

with a Foreword by
Dr David Cesarani

VALLENTINE MITCHELL
LONDON

First published in 1996 in Great Britain by
VALLENTINE MITCHELL & CO. LTD.
Newbury House, 900 Eastern Avenue
London IG2 7HH, England

and in the United States of America by
VALLENTINE MITCHELL
c/o ISBS, 5804 N.E. Hassalo Street, Portland, Oregon 97213-3644

British Library Cataloguing in Publication Data

Beckman, Morris
    Hackney Crucible
    I. Title
    942.15004924

    ISBN 0-85303-286-6

Library of Congress Cataloging-in-Publication Data

Beckman, Morris.
    The Hackney crucible / Morris Beckman.
        p.   cm.
    ISBN 0-85303-286-6 (pbk.)
        1. Jews—England—London—Social conditions. 2. Hackney (London,
    England—Ethnic relations. 3. London (England)—Ethnic relations.
    I. Title.
    DS135.E55L6625   1996
    942.1'004924—dc20   95-17505
                                                                        CIP

Typeset by Vitaset, Paddock Wood, Kent
Printed by Redwood Books, Trowbridge, Wiltshire

Contents

List of Illustrations

Foreword

The years between the two world wars, when Morris Beckman was born and grew up, were a period of transition and crisis for British Jews. This outstanding memoir of Jewish life in London in the 1920s and 1930s captures in microcosm the upheavals that altered the face of Anglo-Jewry.

Morris Beckman was born in Hackney in 1921 and grew up in a house on Amhurst Road, one of the arteries running through a district that was heavily settled by Jews in the years just before and after the First World War. Like his parents, most of the Jews in London at this time had arrived in Britain in the 1890s and 1900s as immigrants from eastern Europe. But restrictions on immigration in 1906 and the 1914–18 War effectively ended the influx. Thereafter, the number of British-born Jews, the children of the immigrants, increased as a proportion of the whole Jewish population. Profound cultural changes followed this demographic shift.

The children of the immigrants, such as Morris and his brothers and sisters, were sundered from their parents by attitudes towards religion, language, culture and politics. Morris's father, along with most of the east European immigrants, was an observant Jew. In a beautiful phrase, Morris observes that for Mr Beckman 'religion was the shield against worries'. Not so for his offspring, who found the sabbath services in Shaklewell Lane synagogue boring and irrelevant. The older Beckmans spoke Yiddish, but their children were raised to be good British citizens speaking only the King's English. For Mr Beckman recreation and religion were interwoven; but his sons liked nothing better than kicking a football around on the Sabbath afternoon. Their enthusiasm for cricket, football, and billiards, followed by their craze for dancing once they were youths, was foreign to the immigrant generation. When faced by anti-Jewish prejudice and organised anti-semitism, young British-born Jews reacted with defiance, whereas their parents, simply grateful to have found a refuge in Britain, tended to lie low and preached a similar policy to their children.

Yet powerful ties still bound together these generations of Jews who were otherwise separated by the place and era in which they were born. This memoir is one of the richest, most intimate portraits of Jewish family and communal life to emerge from the 'crucible' of London Jewry between the wars. Morris describes the domestic routine with a sharp and humorous eye. He observes everything from the joys of Monday washday, to the character of the lodgers. Mary the maid, we learn, was a Christian from Tyneside who followed a well-worn path trodden by many girls from the depressed north-east who came south to work in domestic service for Jews. She picked up Yiddish phrases and spoke them with a Geordie accent.

Morris enables us to enter the childhood world of Jewish boys and girls. He records the games they played, the hunt for sweets, card-swapping and conker tournaments. He describes the bar mitzvah ceremony, the rite of passage for Jewish boys aged thirteen, in which he acquitted himself with distinction. In fact, thanks to his aptitude for Hebrew, his hard work in *cheder*, the Jewish supplementary school, and his curiousity about the 'old country', Morris developed a rapport with his otherwise reserved father. Notwithstanding the pull of secular delights and the alienating character of anglicised Judaism, he retained an affection and respect for his ancestral faith. Several

of the most lyrical passages in this often poetic book recall the
Jewish festivals and the rhythm they gave to the passing years.
September was 'a month of intense gravitational ambiance,
pulling us back to the tree of Judaism'. When Morris served
in the merchant navy during the war, weeks passed before
hunger finally compelled him to breach the Jewish dietary
laws and eat the routine breakfast of bacon and eggs.

Food was central to the life of the Beckman family and the
author marvels at his mother's capacity to cook and feed her
tribe. She was of the old school, but Morris's sisters were
ambitious to strike out in new directions. Interleaved with this
account of his own life, he records how his sisters wrestled
with the competing demands of tradition and ambition. For
Jewish women, too, these were years of transition.

Politics are always in the background. After the First World
War Jews in Britain faced waves of anti-semitism in the form
of anti-alienism, anti-Bolshevism, and anti-Zionism. During
the 1920s the Imperial Fascist League was the focal point
for anti-Jewish agitators. It was superseded in the 1930s by
the much larger, more potent and threatening British Union
of Fascists (BUF). British Jews could not agree on the best
response to Fascism in Britain. Should the Jewish community
as an organised body square up to the BUF? Or should they
rely on the forces of law and order to protect them? The
auguries from Germany after 1933 did not encourage the latter
course. Yet the official leadership of the Jewish community
discouraged any formal political response and even tried to
prevent counter-demonstrations. Consequently, young Jews
like Morris were drawn to left-wing parties which had adopted
an anti-Fascist platform. Others became Zionists, seeing the
creation of a Jewish state as the only sensible response to
anti-semitism. Morris gives a delightful account of the early
activities of the *Habonim* movement which combined scouting
with a Jewish nationalist agenda.

Mr Beckman rather disapproved of *Habonim* since it kept

Morris from his school work. After attending the local primary school, Morris attended the remarkable Hackney Downs school, known as 'The Grocers'. He ranks as another of its distinguished Jewish alumni alongside Lord Goodman, the economist Lord Peston, playwrights Harold Pinter and Steven Berkoff, nutritionist Professor John Yudkin and and historian Professor Geoffrey Alderman. Sadly, the Jewish schoolboys in the 1930s were not allowed to concentrate single-mindedly on their academic work. The struggle between the Republicans and the followers of Franco in Spain, the plight of German Jews under Nazism and the activity of local Fascists were a constant distraction. They asked themselves: 'could it happen here?' To ensure that it did not, Morris and his friends made their contribution to the fight against Fascism by scrapping with Mosleyites on street corners and using catapults to snipe at Blackshirts during BUF rallies. The whole family celebrated news of the set-back suffered by Mosley at the 'Battle of Cable Street' in the East End in October 1936. The final show-down only came in 1939, however. It is striking that Morris, his brothers, and almost all his friends joined the war effort as soon as they could. Many distinguished themselves; tragically, a large number did not come back. Morris Beckman himself served as a wireless operator on merchant vessels and survived being torpedoed. The two world wars cut a swathe through this memoir.

The Hackney Crucible has an epic quality. It documents the saga of one family and, through it, a community. It begins with the immigrant parents hailing from Vilna and the Pale of Settlement, and ends in St Johns Wood, West Hampstead and Golders Green. We see tailors, joiners and small businessmen emerging from the 1914–18 war determined to give their children a good education and prospects. We watch as they enter school, consuming knowledge with a ferocity known only to the children of immigrants, pushing forward into new occupations and the professions. The north London streets, the clubs and playgrounds where young Jews grew to maturity, were the crucible in which a new British Jewish identity was forged. It differed from the religion-based sense of Jewishness typified by the immigrants, but it was no less infused with Jewish tradition and, in certain ways, was actually more assertive. As the Fascists 'turned up the heat' old identities dissolved and new ones formed, to be burnished finally by the war years.

After 1945, the Jewish population of Hackney began to follow the first areas of settlement, Whitechapel and Stepney, into decline. Jewish families became more dispersed than ever before; the immigrant generation was disappearing. However, in Morris Beckman's memoir of these turbulent years Jewish Hackney will live on. *The Hackney Crucible* will take its place beside other classic evocations of Jewish childhood and youth in London, such as Willy Goldman's *East End My Cradle* and Emanuel Litvinoff's *Journey Through a Small Planet*. It is also a tribute to the immigrants: those remarkable mothers and fathers and the vibrant families they created. Such families were, in their own way, also the matrix for a new generation of British Jews. This memoir lovingly captures the life of one such household. It does more. Beckman writes that 'centuries of tradition had etched the pattern of family life'. In recalling that domestic scene he preserves for future generations the impression made by Jewish history on one Jewish family that is, in so many ways, the typical experience of a whole generation and an entire community.

David Cesarani
May 1995

Preface

During the two decades between the World Wars I grew up in the London Borough of Hackney, one of its small but effervescent Jewish community. They were the golden years of the Jew who touched down *en passage* in that bubbling interfusing melting pot.

Materially, we had so much less. Heads of families, burdened by many children, fought against the never-ending troughs of recession to keep their heads above water. It was no wonder they looked old at 40 and were lucky to be alive to enjoy their 60s. Families were argumentative, emotional and raddled with crisis. But they held together and were always supportive when support was needed.

Even during the harassing days of the 1930s when gangs of uniformed British Nazis white-washed slogans like 'Rubinstein go back to Palestine' and 'Perish Judah' on walls and windows and verbally abused and molested Jewish passers-by, there were fewer furrowed brows and more genuine laughter. Errand boys struggling to make distance with heavy duty bicycles supporting capacious iron carriers, laden with groceries, would whistle cheery hit tunes. If they recognised you they called out a cheery 'Wotcha'. Today, if a happy soul whistles in the street he is stared at.

By the early 1920s the more successful Polish and Russian Jewish immigrants who had made a bit had progressed from the dockside slums towards the greener areas of Hackney,

Clapton, Stoke Newington and Stamford Hill. They moved into tranquil tree-lined roads and streets, into terraces of large multi-roomed Victorian and Georgian houses. Not only were they blessed with the luxury of front and back gardens but families no longer had to sleep three, four, even five in a bedroom. It was worth working fingers to the bone for, and this they did.

I cannot recollect a single one of those immigrants, my parents' contemporaries, who had qualified in a secular profession. Any natural zest for academic achievement had been drained by the flight from persecution and then when they reached England the effort to acclimatise and make a living. Made wary by bad experiences and the irrational hostility whence they fled, they introverted and socialised only with their co-religionists. They conversed in their native German, Polish, Russian, Lithuanian and Latvian but their main lingua franca was Yiddish. As a result many could only speak fractured English until the day they died.

Centuries of tradition had etched indelibly the pattern of family life. The man was the breadwinner. His word and desires were law. The wife raised children and made a traditional Jewish home. Sons were ear-marked for academic and professional achievements. Daughters were expected to emulate their mothers and perpetuate the relentless drudgery imposed by the rigidity of Judaic tradition. I recall the hushed condemnations of girls who had rebelled against convention and set out to make careers for themselves, braving intense paternal anger.

By and large the sons, urged on by a burning ambition not to follow their fathers into the family sweatshops producing textiles, furniture, leather goods, clothing and shoes, studied as if their lives depended upon success. Inevitably, this British-born generation produced a plethora of academic, professional and vocational achievers. Medics were the Gods. The Jewish mother running frantically to and fro on Brighton beach and screaming, 'My son, the doctor, is drowning. Please save him' was no idle joke. The successes of sons gave many parents who had known nothing else except hard-work and anxiety the one great pride in their lives.

The community, individualists to a man, threw up a rich sprinkling of eccentrics, non-conformists and black sheep. I remember those warm summer evenings when the air was heavy and still and the sudden explosion of a family quarrel floated across the back gardens to receptive ears and Dad would smile, 'So, the open air Yiddish theatre is playing in Amhurst Road tonight.'

Honesty was everywhere, taken for granted. During warm weather street doors were left wide open allowing neighbour to call into neighbour for coffee and a gossip. Every household could produce a limitless supply of home-made butter biscuits and strudels. As others pub-crawled, we boys biscuit-crawled. From house to house, never being refused. Owners of cars seldom bothered to lock them not even overnight. Poverty then was not regarded as an excuse to steal. Eyes were averted from embarrassing family upsets but seldom from anyone genuinely needing help.

In our stretch of Amhurst, between its junctions with Sandringham Road and Downs Park Road, the Clarfelts, Cohens, Galinskys, Beckmans, Corals, Rappaports, Peppermans and other large families mingled freely, argumentatively, helpfully, excitedly. Merely existing was banned. Life was seen and heard to be lived.

Although the first listed burial of a Jew in Hackney occurred in 1656, when the wardens of Katherine Creechurch buried a Domingo de Brito, a Sephardi, whose parents had fled the Spanish Inquisitorial choice of conversion or being burnt alive at the stake, it was in 1688 that Hackney recorded its first Jewish settler. His name was Isaac Alvarez, a jeweller, whose parents had also fled from the Inquisition.

He was a senior warden in the Mahamad, an Executive body set up in 1657 to administer to the sparse Jewish communities in London and the city's outlying villages. Its power was absolute. This led inevitably to its being accused of acting with more vigour than compassion. But it did give the scattered Jewish families a sense of community. Anti-semitism did not then exist in its later more virulent forms and Jews were regarded merely as being people of a different persuasion. Appreciating this tolerance the Mahamad came down heavily on behaviour and commercial malpractices that could have created public prejudice.

In 1694 Alvarez bought a modest dwelling in Homerton for his two children, Deborah and Abraham, from Sir Edward de Carteret, a Gentleman Usher in Ordinary to His Majesty. In 1698 he sold the property and moved, and from then until 1716 when rating began, there were no further records of Jewish settlement in Hackney. But, it must have existed because in 1715 the Vicar of Hackney noted an order at a vestry meeting requiring Jews to pay burial fees for their dead. Until Jews acquired their first cemetery in Mile End it was not known how and where Jewish pedlars and travellers passing through Hackney were buried.

Alvarez was a settler, not an itinerant. He surfaced again when a fire gutted his home and he moved to Mare Street, to find that two Jewish families had preceded him there. Their heads were Moses Silva and Jacob Cohen. An outgoing personality, Benjamin da Costa, who was regularly elected to parish office and just as regularly paid the customary fine to avoid it, was the next to join them.

At that time Hackney was just far enough away from the city to avoid the soot that prevailing winds blew to blight the nearer Bethnal Green. Hackney's verdant fields were spattered with livestock. The air was clean. Its residents enjoyed the country pursuits of riding, walking, fishing and boating in the River Lee. Its attractions drew in the famous and the wealthy who erected impressive residences set amidst spacious gardens.

Among them were the first affluent Jewish families. They trailed in their wake the first Jewish poor, beggars like Benjamin da Costa, a destitute wax chandler, who received charity for ten years. Even so at the end of the eighteenth century Hackney could count no more than an estimated 25 Jewish families.

The first half of the nineteenth century witnessed an influx of the mainly wealthier Jewish families settling in Hackney and at one period every member of the Jewish Legislative Council lived there. Social contact with Gentile neighbours remains an area of speculation but we do know that in 1800 the ladies of Hackney allowed Jewish ladies into their subscription library and that the Misses Henrietta and Ella Levin and a Miss Levy were elected to the Hackney singing classes. There arrived that redoubtable man of letters, Solomon Mendes, who seldom left his house in Clapton and yet maintained an incessant flow of correspondence to a wide-ranging circle. He was joined by A. Nunes who published with John Thompson in 1798 the brilliantly illustrated volume entitled *Botany Displayed*.

Word spread about the charm of Hackney. Early in the nineteenth century Nathan Meyer Rothschild bought the lease of a villa with eight acres in Stamford Hill. His sister, married to Abraham Montefiore, bought a house in Kingsland Road. Joel Emanuel, a Bond Street jeweller, moved into Rothschild's house. He was quickly followed by Abraham Solomons, a city retailer of hats and silk gloves; by Solomon Israel, a ship-broker; by the Brandons and that most sociable of bachelors, Benjamin de Moses de Elias de Lindon, who was a member of both Lloyds and the Stock Exchange. Jewish writers and academics made their way to Hackney; the writer Grace Aguilar, Miriam Belisario, author of the acclaimed *Sabbath Evening at Home*, Jacob Rodrigues Peynardo who wrote learned articles for the first American Jewish magazine, entitled *The Occident*, and Elias Lindo, the pioneer Anglo-Jewish historian.

A stabilising middle class trickled in comprising merchants, artisans, workers and clerical staff. There was Lyon Abrahams, a second-hand clothes dealer; Joel Benjamin, watchmaker; Samuel Avila, pawnbroker; Joseph Delville, bookseller; George Dias, city auctioneer and Michael Barnett and his sister, a dressmaker.

In 1842 William Robinson noted 'The village of Hackney has been selected for retirement by that respectable class in society, the Jews. But at this time there are very few of that persuasion in the parish.'

Yet, gargantuan changes were picking up speed, pushed along by new inventions, by the momentous expansion of industrialisation and a steep increase in population. The insatiable demand from the Empire for British-manufactured goods combined with the advantageous inflow of cheap raw materials from that same Empire were strengthening London's status as the financial and commercial hub of the world. There developed a voracious appetite for land upon which to build factories, offices, dwellings and administrative centres of all kinds. The city rolled outwards in all directions. It greedily swallowed dozens of villages, Hackney among them, and covered fields and farms under oceans of bricks and tarmac in a higgledy-piggledy development that forever afterwards has bedevilled London's traffic.

With all their thrust for prosperity the Victorians displayed one saving grace. They created many parks and squares and to this day if you view through half-closed eyes on a hot summer's day selected spots over Hackney Downs or one of the great parks, Victoria, Clissold or Finsbury, you can visualise how idyllic the countryside of Hackney once was.

Late into the nineteenth century the number of Jews in Hackney remained comparatively few. It was a scene that changed perceptibly when the explosive turn-of-the-century exodus of Jews fleeing the implacable hostility and pogroms of Eastern Europe spilled its quotas of the hungry, the impoverished and the bewildered onto the quaysides of London's Thames. Among those hapless refugees were my mother, Rebecca Harris, and my father, Joseph Harris Beckman.

On 15 October 1904 they were married at the New Road synagogue in London's East End.

Introduction

I wrote *The Hackney Crucible* to record the melding of immigrant Jews into the British way of life during the two decades between the World Wars. London's East End is the locale of the book. It concerns that turn-of-the-century influx of refugees from East European pogroms, including my parents, who quickly knuckled down to fighting their way from penniless disorientation to hardship, to poverty and, by the late 1920s, to a level of comfort those they had left behind could never have dreamed of achieving. By and large the immigrants were accepted by the resident population. There were the inevitable abrasions caused by what Professor James Parkes of Oxford, who made a study of racial intolerance, percipiently dubbed the dislike of the unlike. But there was no menacing targeting of an ethnic minority for political reasons until Sir Oswald Mosley came onto the scene when he launched his British Union of Fascists on 1 October 1932 in Great George Street, London. He copied Hitler's contempt for democracy, his uniforms, his slogans and above all his propaganda. Mosley and top-ranking British fascists like Raven Thomson, Oliver Leese and William Joyce became friendly with leading Nazis like Josef Goebbels and Julius Streicher and learned lessons from their successful masters.

The brave new world promised by politicians after the First World War had never materialised. With the lowering shadows from that unforgettable bloodbath merging with the early storm clouds presaging the coming World War those were relentlessly depressing years. Throughout Europe poverty and unemployment without an end in sight created a bitter mood which manifested itself in riots, strikes and demonstrations. Inevitably, the mood developed a wide ugly streak. Naturally, someone had to be to blame; anyone, so long as there was someone. Historically those in power, seeking it, coveting it, have always required a scapegoat to divert blame away from themselves. The ideal scapegoat was always a high-profile ethnic minority in no position to defend itself. Thus, enter on stage, from left or right, no matter, the ever-available sacrifice, the Jews.

Up to the middle of the nineteenth century the Jews were the sole prominent minority in most European countries. They were defenceless. Because they were generally successful they were envied. They were there. After 1950 the Blacks and Asians poured into Britain, the North Africans into France and Italy, the Italians and Yugoslavs into Switzerland, the Turks into Germany and third world migrants into every labour-hungry booming European country. But before they arrived in sufficient numbers to share the flak it was always the Jews who were the culprits for all ills. The Germans, refusing to accept that their vaunted military machine had been defeated in battle, blamed the Jews for having stabbed the Fatherland in the back. One wonders how the thousands of Jews who died fighting for The Fatherland managed to stab themselves in the back. The answer is that there is nothing a brain-washed mind cannot bring itself to believe. Not even in England.

After that same war malicious tongues spread the rumours that while British boys died in the trenches the Jews had waxed fat at home. Overall the British public, sophisticated with the checks and balances evolved by centuries of democracy, ignored the calumnies. However, stung to answer, the Rev. Michael Adler DSO BA, produced a book four inches thick entitled simply *The British Jewry Roll of Honour*, printed by the Caxton Publishing Company. Winston Churchill, then Secretary of State for War, and Field Marshall Earl Haig, KT, were among those who praised the Jewish war effort. Viscount Northcliff pointed out in the same book 'Although the Jewish population of the Empire is comparatively small Jewry has to its credit 5 Victoria Crosses, 50 Distinguished Service Orders, 242 Military Crosses, 80 Distinguished Conduct Medals, 308 Military Medals and 374 Mentioned In Despatches. 9,000 in the British army alone fell in action or were wounded and missing.'

All in all, the Jews integrated easily into the East End. It was not a hostile environment like the one they had fled from, and until Mosley stoked the fires of racism, anti-semitism was on a personal basis where someone simply disliked Jews. My father and his contemporaries made no bones that they were lucky to have reached England and were grateful for it. But, to the end of their days, they kept themselves to themselves socially. My father, who spoke Polish, Russian, German and Yiddish fluently, never really mastered the English language. There were many like him. They were paranoic about one thing, that their sons would through education achieve great heights. Well, many did. But in the early 1930s when, for the first time, British-born Jews exceeded immigrant Jews, the fissures between the mainly devout parents and their children appeared and widened. The immigrants were almost to a man deeply religious. All life, outside of their work or businesses revolved around their synagogues and Judaic custom and tradition. Inevitably, their children pulled away in all directions from the Judaic tree and traumas and disputes gave the famed tight Jewish family unit an irretrievable shock. Yet, despite the hundreds of family dramas being played out the community could unify and face outwards against outside threat. The immigrants were Jews who lived in England. Their children were British whose faith was Jewish. But in the 1930s when the Jewish refugees from Nazi terror started to arrive and the depredations of the Blackshirts who, by their rampaging through East End streets after dark, virtually imposed a curfew on elderly Jews who were too afraid to venture out, the dichotomy between parents and sons dissolved.

My book on The 43 Group was published soon after completion of *The Hackney Crucible*. Invitations to speak about The 43 Group and British Fascism rolled in. I spoke to a variety of organisations in various places. Quite a number were to Jewish cultural societies where audiences comprised mainly pensioners. Their memories of the Blackshirts in the 1930s evoked very deep feelings. They had no illusions as to what would have happened to them had Mosley got into power. But, they had no idea of what would have happened to them had the Nazis invaded and conquered England after Dunkirk.

Fascism can only exist by hating. It is nourished by it. Without hate it withers and dies. It was the only creed which, under the cloak of patriotism, targeted an ethnic minority to gain political support regardless of the distress and worse it would bring down on the chosen scapegoat. When Mosley launched his British Union of Fascists he achieved two firsts; he was the first Englishman who built up and would have presented a ready-made fifth column to the enemy of his country should that enemy have invaded and won, and, secondly, he was the first Englishman to have deliberately indoctrinated decent young men who joined his Party for patriotic motives into hating a section of his countrymen. This poisoning of minds took place in the headquarters of the BUF when they moved to the massive Black House in Kings Road. These young men were made to read anti-semitic literature. They had to attend Goebbels-like lectures where Jews were metamorphosised into rats, lice, vermin and all creatures nasty. The true-blue Aryan Blackshirts were, of course, linked with noble beasts like lions, tigers and elephants. Then, they went out to guard fascist orators who warned their audiences about the Great Jewish Conspiracy to rule the world and all that nonsense. The British fascists who visited their Nazi masters had learned their lessons well. This resulted in endless acts of violence by fascists against the Jews especially during the three years leading up to the outbreak of war.

There were evenings when I could not walk from my home in Amhurst Road and be able to find a way to my destination without encountering a Blackshirt meeting. There were so many. If my friends and I wore our schoolcaps and blazers we received some hard looks but were left alone. Nevertheless, if one often went out at night time, as I did, things could happen. One rainy autumn evening I was walking along Stoke Newington High Street when I spotted about 20 Blackshirts obviously coming away from a meeting. They were marching in step, in fours, military fashion, and singing their favourite tune, the Nazi anthem the *Horst Wessel*. I hurried into a deep shop doorway and crouched in the darkness, back pressed into a corner. They passed yards away singing the English version to a Nazi lyric 'When SS knives slit Jewish throats'. Friends experienced similar happenings. Fortunately, after their meetings, hyped up, they would sing noisily and you could hear the martial tramp of their feet from a distance.

Yet, the Jewish community carried on with their integrating, fully participating in social, sporting and all types of public communal activities. Families bubbled and boiled with cultural upheavals and we all went out to those wonderful clubs for boys and girls like Brady, Oxford and St. Georges, Stamford Hill, Hackney West Central and others. A great comfort was the friendships many of us had made with Gentiles and the overall public's hatred of Mosley's fascists. They always had a bad press. They were rather loathed and their outdoor meetings were quite often attacked by anti-fascists. Their worst and most active enemies were the communists.

It was put about in the 1930s by the fascists and their sympathisers that there was a Machiavellian Judeo–Bolshevik conspiracy to rule the world. All Jews were communists and all communists were Jews or, if they were not, they could be counted as Jews. The surprising fact is how few Jews in the 1930s actually joined the communists. Jews are individualists and non-conformists to a man. They shy away from anything totalitarian. They did so even in London's East End where they saw the communists disrupting and fighting the fascists, they would cheer on the former and even dive in to support them. The fascists were the enemy. That was that. The Spanish Civil War polarised attitudes throughout the East End and even those Jews who were almost anti-communist came down heavily on the side of the Spanish Republicans. It was a relief for many young Jews to be able to attack the fascists alongside the communists or anti-fascists despite their Board of Deputies' injunctions to steer clear of trouble and not get involved in street violence. This caused even further rifts in Jewish families. The immigrants whose childhood memories evoked their fears and terrors when drunken Cossacks or peasants roamed the ghetto quarters for Jews to beat up sided with the caution of the Establishment. Their sons, born into a free and tolerant society, resented both the rampaging Blackshirts and their community leaders' counsels. Sow the wind and reap the whirlwind. Many of those Jewish East London schoolboys who went off to war and returned as trained battle-hardened veterans could not wait to join The 43 Group, which from 1946 to 1950, attacked the emergent post-war Mosleyite Union Movement with such a devastating ferocity, and destroyed it.

The 43 Group was a spontaneous phenomenon representing probably the only time in Jewish history since the Romans destroyed the temple in 180 AD and scattered Jewish survivors to everywhere, that in peacetime in a diaspora country Jews turned on their tormentors in an organised disciplined body and attacked them and wiped them out. It happened in London.

Introduction

In November 1944 the first fascist outdoor meeting since the war broke out took place at Speakers Corner, Hyde Park. The legend on the platform bore the words 'The British League of Ex-servicemen and women'. The speakers were Jeffrey Hamm and Victor Burgess, both pre-war BUF officers. Both had been interned under Clause 18*b* in the Emergency Power Bill, the clause that enabled the Home Secretary to imprison suspected enemies of the State. Their speeches were anti-democratic, anti-semitic and castigated the politicians for fighting against the wrong people. At this moment British troops were fighting their way into Germany against the said wrong people. The meeting went off quietly. Mosley heard the result and metaphorically rubbed his hands with joy. He set about the resurrection of the BUF. It would now be called the Union Movement. It started well, so well, that the confident Mosley told the *News Chronicle* in an interview in 1946 that his experience had not only confirmed his views but had intensified them. The fact that some 55 million Europeans had lost their lives in the war started by his creed bothered him not at all. In 1947–49 when Mosley's Unionists started to come over to members of The 43 Group with their hands up palms outwards saying that they were leaving the Union Movement and wanted to talk to us, Group members would go with them for coffees or to a pub. And how those fascists, or rather ex-fascists, talked. It was as if they were getting things off their chests. We learned many things but the most chilling was the most obvious. At the time of Dunkirk when everyone thought that the Nazis would invade and almost certainly conquer England the die-hard Blackshirts in the internment camps waxed jubilant. They could only talk about how they would help their Nazi masters to render Britain Jew-free, what positions of power they would be given under their German masters, 'Gauleiter of Golders Green always raised a great laugh' and how they would share out the loot left behind by the gas-chambered British Jews.

These were the men who, after London's East End streets had enjoyed six peaceful years without trouble and violence, came back to those same streets and once again poured out their anti-democratic and anti-semitic rantings. Jewish ex-servicemen coming home from the war were outraged. The more war-weary slipped back into civvy street, but others were galvanised into action. They urged their MPs and then their own Board of Deputies to put a halt to this unbelievable obscenity. But, in vain. The ex-servicemen realised that the Jewish Defence Committee of the Board had to be a responsible law-abiding body and no matter how great the provocation they could not condone any action that would break the country's laws. Therefore, their calls for restraint among Jews in the 1930s carried weight. It was mostly, not always, heeded. But the post-war situation was different. The Holocaust had happened. For Jews everywhere it had changed everything and the Establishment's pleadings for calm and biting the bullet fell on stony ground. Thirty-eight ex-servicemen and five ex-servicewomen convened a meeting in Maccabi House, West Hampstead. It was the first week in March 1946. They formed The 43 Group. Its aims were two-fold; to expose the post-war fascists and to destroy them. They succeeded in doing both. The 43 Group, which had peaked at 900 active members and could have enrolled thousands more, both Jewish and Gentile ex-servicemen, disbanded in March 1950. Throughout its vicious no-quarter war with the Union Movement the Jewish Defence Committee, in common with the fascists, wanted it to disappear. What the Establishment did not see or, perhaps, did not want to see, was the tremendous support The Group had from the Jewish community at large, from the British press which totally condemned the Union Movement and the government for permitting it to happen, and from the London judiciary who bent over backwards to be lenient with The Group members brought before them by the police and from the general public.

Thus, 18 years after Mosley launched his British Union of Fascists headed by a charismatic leader, bolstered by hundreds of disciplined officers and with a detailed manifesto for his planned Corporate State, it ceased to exist and British Fascism became history. A substantial proportion of The 43 Group commandos who hammered the Union carapace of street thugs into submission and surrender had never forgotten the insults and the fears that these same thugs had imposed on them and their families ten years earlier. Revenge was sweet.

Perhaps because human nature is itself unchanging history repeats itself.

The *Jewish Chronicle* of 2 October 1936 carried an unusual advertisement. It was large and in bold thick black type and in a panel prominently placed. It urged all Jews to keep away from the East End the coming Sunday because the British Union of Fascists were going to hold a big parade. The advertisement had been placed by the Jewish Establishment. How wrong they were. How short-sighted. Even, how cowardly.

The parade that took place or, rather, was stopped from taking place on that Sunday 4 October became known as The Battle of Cable Street. Over 7,000 southern-English uniformed fascists assembled at Tower Hill early that day. They were going to march in four separate contingents behind their bands, Union Jacks and fascist banners to four separate points in the heart of Jewish East End. Mosley planned to speak at each stop. Over 6,000 foot police and the entire mounted police force in the East End lined the proposed route to the boulevard-wide gateway into the Jewish areas, Commercial Road. Large assemblies of police waited at strategic points in case they were needed. They were. It was provocation and intimidation on a massive scale. If the fascists had succeeded in their plans their stock would have risen very high. Also, if they had succeeded the Jewish and anti-fascist residents would have provided open season for rampaging vicious fascist gangs. The government refused to act. The role of the police was to protect free speech, hence they were out to protect the fascists. The Board of Deputies? In fairness they almost certainly would have made no impact on the government had they tried to get them to ban the march. But, what they should have done was to have exhorted all able-bodied Jews to turn out and join the other anti-fascists in defending their co-religionists. Instead, they did the opposite.

However, the British working classes saw the rabbit. They knew deep down in their gut that it had to be stopped and they turned up trumps. It was estimated that 70,000 anti-fascists converged on the East End. There were dockers, South Wales miners, Tyneside shipyard and steel workers. There were trade unionists, communists, white collar workers and several thousand Jews who were sick and ashamed of keeping their heads down. From the early hours of that Sunday they were building the barricades across Commercial Road and the alternative route at Cable Street. Cars, vans, carts, baulks of timber, furniture, dustbins, debris from building sites, everything went into the barricades. They stretched deeply back. Time and again the police charged the Commercial Road barricade to break a pathway through for the waiting fascists. They failed. As one protester was hurt or arrested another stepped forward and took his place. Casualties and arrests were many. The police then tried to break through Cable Street to allow the march. By now they were angry and frustrated. The fighting became vicious on both sides and again casualties ran high. But, they could not get through. The Commissioner of Police told Mosley to cancel the march, which he did.

The effect on the fascists was devastating. The anticipated gold of a triumphant day turned into dross. That morning proved to be the highwater mark of the British Union of Fascists' hubris and arrogance. The very moment that the police were forced to order Mosley to call off his great parade the tide began to recede. The sound-hearted British working class had given authority a clear message. The excessive depravities of British Fascism would not be tolerated. The government got the message. It very quickly introduced a Public Order Act banning all political uniforms. This struck a bad psychological blow at the fascists. The smart uniforms had been a major attraction for young men to join it. It gave the wearers a unified comradely feeling. The Sunday after the Battle of Cable Street some 300 fascists ran pell-mell down Whitechapel. They were in vicious mood and broke Jewish shop windows and attacked any man or woman who they thought looked Jewish. But, they could not help seeing slogans whitewashed on the walls proclaiming 'They did not pass'. These replaced the pre-4 October slogans which had declared 'They shall not pass'.

During my talks I still get a warm glow when a pensioner comes up to me and says that he was at the Battle of Cable Street and that he had been fighting the fascists in the 1930s and 1940s sandwiching his service in the armed forces against the German Nazis and Japanese. After my talk to a JACS meeting one feisty old boy came up to me and said 'You know, in the Thirties and Forties we were both fighting the fascists and . . .' he added with a grin 'The Board of Deputies. Well, we saw them both off.'

Chapter One

On 21 February 1921 I was born during the early hours of the morning at home, at 147 Amhurst Road, Hackney, London E8. My parents had settled for five but in those pre-coil, pre-pill years mistakes did occur quite frequently and so I made my unplanned appearance. I was the youngest of six; Sam, the eldest, then sister Rose, then Michael, then Freda, then Aubrey and finally the error, me.

Few Jews have been fortunate enough to have survived several generations in one tolerant climate which is why family trees are rare and curiosity in ancestry remains pragmatically non-existent. The only grandparent I vaguely remember was my maternal grandmother, reputed to have been an iron disciplinarian with a heart of gold and a protective spot for the family runt, me. I have one treasured photograph of her taken in 1902 with her five daughters; my mother Rebecca and aunts Rose, Hanna, Tamara and Golda. Golda was the much sat-upon youngest. The other three grandparents I never knew.

My mother was born in Vilna, Poland. My father never talked about his origins. Their children showed a surprising lack of curiosity and asked no questions. This malaise affected all my British-born contemporaries. No questions asked. No reminiscences. A sad loss.

With the passage of time Christians who emigrated from Europe to the new lands succumbed to a comforting amnesia.

1

They remembered only what was best and sweetest in the old country, forgetting the miseries that had made them emigrate. This self-delusion helped them to retain a grass roots identity. By and large Jews fled from infernos of pogroms and persecution imposed upon them purely because they had been born into the Jewish faith. To the ignorant, every Jew had killed Christ. The lands whence they escaped were abominations. They never wanted to talk about them, think about them. The wandering Jew of mythology, driven from country to country, actually existed.

It was inescapable that one day, one century, this suffering would germinate the seeds of Zionism and raise visionaries like Theodor Herzl. Shocked by the intellectual anti-semitism that surfaced in France over the Dreyfus Affair Herzl concluded that Jews would only ever be free in their own country and this land could only be the land they had been driven from by the Romans around 180 AD. Israelis, today, with all their being surrounded by overwhelming numbers of hostile Arabs, exude a self-confidence denied their diaspora co-religionists because they are rooted in their own soil.

Our house was always clean and smelling of resinous polishes. Our maids all came from Tyneside. On duty they wore neat black dresses fronted by stiffly starched white pinafores. They worked hard alongside my mother as equals and with my two sisters as chattering conspirators. They had their own room at the top of the house with its own landing outside. Black and white checkerboard linoleum covered both floors. It was highly waxed and when the sun shone onto it through the large sash windows it became warm and pliant, a sensual delight to crawl upon.

After lunch the maids would retire to their penthouse floor and enjoy an afternoon's rest and privacy. They were regarded as members of the family, ate the same food and had free run of house and garden. They kept their distance but not in a servile manner. There was a demarcation across which we

2

would never intrude, nor would the maids. Egalitarianism had not then reared its ugly head.

My earliest memory. We were in the kitchen. The sun poured through the large sash windows. Present were one of my brothers and Mary Kenny, an ebullient Irish-Tyneside maid. For the first time I walked, unaided, without falling, from one wall across the linoleum to the other wall, where I collapsed. It had seemed such a long journey, never ending. I remember being scooped up by Mary amidst excited shouts.

Amhurst Road was a long through road running from Stoke Newington in the north-east to its south-easterly end where Mare Street began. It was a gently curving wide residential road with sensibly wide pavements. Our house was in the section between its junction with Sandringham Road, wherein nestled the Mitford Tavern pub, and the cross-roads where Downs Park Road ran across it. Motorised traffic was sparse enough for us boys to play football and cricket in season in the road. Cricket was favourite. If a batsman hit a sorbo ball (a solid rubber, hard bouncy ball) into a front garden, it was a four. If the ball hit a house above the first floor windows it was a six. If a ball broke a window we all ran. It got so that no one boy would provide a ball. So, we all chipped in with farthings and halfpennies to make a joint purchase. Then, it was God help the unrestrained idiot who did put it through a window. Passers-by would gape at clusters of boys up-ending a culprit and dropping him when coins fell from his trouser pockets onto the pavement.

Our sector of Amhurst Road sported facing rows of tall, five-floored terraced brick houses. The front gardens were well-tended and richly green with bushes and trees. During the 1930s they were useful for hiding behind when Mosley's blackshirts, on a high after a meeting or rally, passed by with bellicose arrogance. They were invaluable for concealing our soccer and cricket bags after we had, in Dad's view, desecrated the Sabbath by having played games on it. Later, my brothers found them useful to duck down behind when girls they did not want to meet passed by.

Our house had a semi-basement area which comprised at the back a scullery and adjoining kitchen. The kitchen was square and spacious. The scullery was a third of its size. It was the working room with gas stove, two sinks, working utensils on rows of hooks. It was dominated by an enormous copper cauldron four feet high and with a yard wide diameter across its open top. It was shaped like an enormous artillery shell with its sharp end firmly embedded into the top of a brick-built stove underneath it.

Every Monday was washing day. Mary and my sisters would rise early and while Mary filled the cauldron with buckets of water and lit the coal fire beneath it, Freda and Rose would sort out the piles of clothing, bed linen, curtains and napery to be laundered. By nine o'clock the cauldron would be boiling away and clouds of steam filled the scullery. The three girls would stream with sweat as they poured soap flakes into the cauldron and stirred its contents with large wooden paddles. They kept the fire glowing with added coal. All internal doors in the house were open and the heat genera-ted flooded up the stairs and throughout the house. In clement weather the four clothes lines running the length of the back lawn were totally taken up with what had been washed. When it rained a system of lines and strings pulled taut criss-crossed every part of the lower part of the house. The jungly thickets of drying washing would drive Dad into the sanctuary of the dining room when he came home from work and my brothers out to anywhere.

That day no meals were cooked in the scullery. We ate plates of sandwiches, fruit, cheese and cakes and drank gallons of tea. Perversely, I loved the excitement of wash Mondays and the red-faced even bawdy good-humour that never flagged.

Around 5 o'clock two ironing tables would be set up in the

kitchen and the two irons, heavy, solid, cast iron, were heated on the gas stove. Using them was strenuous work. Soon the washing, neatly folded in squares and rectangles, would be piling up. Mum, barred by the girls from helping in this arduous work, heated up her nourishing bone-stock soups and made sandwiches. While the girls stacked the ironed laundry in the very large airing cupboard any boys handy would be roped in to empty and clean the copper cauldron until it gleamed. Sometimes the work did not finish before 10 o'clock at night. Nobody wanted to leave any work for the morrow. It was accepted that the girls could sleep in late and the boys would have to get their own breakfasts. That was the idea. But every Tuesday morning would see Mum down early cooking scrambled egg and toast breakfasts, ignoring our selfishly weak protests. The legendary Jewish mother had her virtues.

The street side of the semi-basement area had one large room, the dining room. It was dead-centred by a magnificent oval mahogany table which had five leaves. The three middle ones could be cranked out and put back in by turning a steel handle that worked the complicated gearing beneath the leaves. Never once did it fail to work. The net curtains were covered by heavy green drapes down to floor level. They matched the four green leather-covered armchairs. In a corner stood an upright Bechstein piano. Rose could read music and often played it. I suffered the illusion that I could sing and would nag her to play *Amapola*, which I sang. When we finished she would say 'That was very nice. No more. Go out and play.' The room had several aspidistras and jungly many-leaved plants among which I indulged in Tarzan fantasies. That room was a sanctuary into which I could go and feel utterly safe.

Across a corridor was the coal cellar, situated beneath half the front garden area. I remember the coalmen with their heavy duty leather aprons covering their shoulders and backs down to their waists. They wore leather-peaked caps back to front and large knee pads. Their heartfelt grunts when they knelt and emptied the contents of their rough canvas sacks through the manhole could be heard all through the house. Despite the door to the cellar being firmly shut during delivery unstoppable tendrils of coal dust would seep into the house and Mary would mutter mutinously as she wiped surfaces with damp cloths that were quickly turned black by the dust.

The echoing call of the coalies announcing their arrival in Amhurst Road could be heard for a long distance. Their hundredweight sacks would be stacked in neat rows upon a sturdy open-sided dray, drawn by two enormous shire horses. They towered over me. I was awed and not a little afraid of those broad-chested massively-muscled beasts. They were, of course, the most gentle of creatures.

The coalies would rat-tat the brass knocker on our lower street door. They were huge muscled men with weathered faces, the human equivalent of their horses. When the coal cellar was emptied by normal consumption by the end of winter it ill behove anyone to leave things in it and forget about them but somehow we all did this. Thus, when the coalies emptied their sacks down the manhole they covered cricket bats, handbags, discarded clothing and other items. The coalies worked at a furious non-stop pace. Once they had started no one dared dart into the cellar to retrieve things.

We paid for so many sackfuls. An unpopular chore for one of my brothers or Mary was to stand by the manhole and ensure that we were not delivered short. The coalies understood this and some commented menacingly about being spied upon. The ones who grumbled about it the most were probably those who supplemented their income by filching the odd sackful of coal. Selling sackfuls of coal for half price for cash presented no problem.

Above the semi-basement was the first floor, about six feet above ground level. It contained my parents' bedroom, a large

6

square room with a high ceiling and enormous windows which overlooked the back garden. It had a common wall with the drawing room, which overlooked the front garden. The drawing room was special, a shrine. We called it Mum's palace. It reeked of all that we were not, class, taste, society. We always obeyed Dad's law and took off our shoes before entering it. The parquet floor was a rich honey colour, without blemish. But, the snook cocked at their nose-to-the-grindstone lives by my parents manifested itself in a glorious suite of chinoiserie furniture. It was delicate but strong, intricately-carved, beautifully patterned and ormolued. It comprised a glass cabinet, filled with silver and glass ornaments, a matching chaise-longue, four chairs, two armchairs and a nest of four tables. Dad loved showing this room and its chinoiserie set to visitors.

July 1945, the war in Europe was over. I was between ships, as I thought, until Marconi Marine informed me that I had had my last posting. I bummed around London at a loose end. Sam had survived as an infantryman with the 8th Army through Africa, Sicily and Italy and was stuck in Ancona attached to the military government of that port. Mick was still stationed at the RAF base in Dorval, near Montreal, and was flying God-knew-where. Aubrey had been demobilised from the RAF. He had married Pat Lannon, an open tournament tennis player. He was busily setting up in partnership with another accountant, Ivor Casson. They were both determined to make up for lost time. This, they did.

Then, late one afternoon, I returned home and heard Mum frantically calling for help. I rushed up to her bedroom and found her trying to lift Dad. He had fallen half out of the bed. The lower half of his body had been entrapped by blankets. I lifted him back onto the bed and phoned our family doctor, a Dr Sachs. He and an ambulance arrived almost at the same moment. He diagnosed a heavy stroke. I had been busy on the phone. Aubrey arrived by taxi. Rose and Harry arrived as Aubrey went off in the ambulance with Dad to the Mildmay Park hospital. Mrs Cohen and daughter, Bessie, came in from next door. Mrs Clarfelt came in from the other side. Sam's wife, Rosamund, appeared and soon the house was full of people. They were sympathetic, commiserating. I sneaked upstairs to get away from them.

Four days later I was alone in the house with Mum. She was in the scullery, cooking. Unexpectedly, she collapsed. She was rushed in an ambulance to the Royal Northern hospital in Holloway. The following morning Aubrey and I went to see her. We were asked to wait in a small reception room near where she was. Suddenly, about 8.00 am, bells rang. Nurses rushed past our open doorway with a doctor in hot pursuit. Aubrey and I rushed out to see them hurry into Mum's room. Aubrey gripped my shoulder and breathed 'It can't be . . . .'

Mum died at that moment. The cause, a burst appendix. Back in the reception room Aubrey and I just stared out of the windows. A doctor came in and muttered the deepest of regrets. A nurse brought in two cups of tea. We left them untouched. For a long time we were in tears and too choked to speak and then Aubrey said 'I'll get a taxi. I'll go straight to Dr Sachs and ask him if I should tell Dad. I'll phone the family and get telegrams away to Sam and Mick. I'll be back as soon as I can. Meanwhile, you stand watch by Mum.'

According to custom a dead Jewish person has to be attended by a Jewish male until burial. Families unwilling or unable to perform this last rite could hire watchers through their synagogues. These were usually elderly men, retired or poor, who needed to earn a bit of extra money. Aubrey saw my hesitation and said emotionally 'No one but us will watch over Mum. No one.'

The matron on that floor was conversant with Jewish custom. She could not have been more understanding. She put a chair beside Mum's bed and told me that I would not be disturbed. But, if I wanted anything, I should ring the bell above the bed. For seven hours I sat on that chair staring at Mum's peaceful profile, holding her hand from time to time, not daring to kiss her, dozing off from time to time and, when realisation struck home, wiping away tears. I was asleep when Aubrey returned. He woke me gently and reported 'Dr Sachs told me to tell Dad. Then, I went home and phoned and sent telegrams to all the family everywhere. That done, I walked to the hospital. I just dreaded facing Dad and telling him and the walk helped me to compose myself. When I did go in to see him, I was tongue-tied. I stared at Dad. He was propped up by pillows. He just looked at me and then he raised his arm in a fending off gesture and he said, "I know. No one has told me. But, I know . . .".'

As Mick stepped off his plane at Dorval, Montreal, after a flight back from Brazil he was handed the telegram. Given immediate compassionate leave he was rushed onto a plane just leaving for the UK and just about made the funeral. Sam could not get away. After Mum was buried in the Jewish cemetery at Edmonton it was evident that Dad, paralysed down one side and with his speech affected, would need constant looking after. Freda and her husband, Hymie, took him into their home at great disruption to themselves. We all contributed money to pay a male nurse to look after Dad until he died, a few years later, of Parkinson's disease.

The funeral and Dad's incapacity splintered the family asunder. None of us wanted to remain in the house in Amhurst Road. Aubrey and Pat had moved into a flat in St. John's Wood. Mick returned to flying for a while and then returned to build up a successful textile merchanting business. Sam, demobilised, came home. He and Mick agreed amicably that they did not have the temperaments to work together so he set up his own business and succeeded beyond everyone's expectations. Rose and Harry moved into a house in The Vale, Golders Green, with their two young daughters. Mick moved into a flat near Baker Street. I slept in the house alone. It became a carcass to be picked clean by vultures. Things just disappeared while I was out during the days. I was aimless. In fits and bursts I would sit down and write stories and send them off. Rejection slips flowed back but sometimes I scored hits and the cheques were welcome. Then, out of the blue I received a phone call from Yorkshire from a Mr J. Peisal. He said that Dad had bought fabrics from his mill during the 1930s, that he had liked my father and was sorry to hear of my family's troubles. He asked me to see him in Leeds. I took the train up north and met him in the lounge of The Queen's Hotel. He told me that his mill produced fine worsted *suitings and was now increasing production to meet the demands from a consumer-hungry world. Before the war he had done a lot of business in Scandinavia. He wanted to resuscitate that business and he wanted me to go there and do it for him. 'Why me?' I protested. 'I've never sold anything and I don't know the first thing about textiles.' 'They're so hungry for goods, you won't need to sell,' assured Peisal. 'I'll give you a list of firms to see, old customers. I'll give you all the details and specifications they will want to know. You see them, show them the samples, answer their questions and just collect the orders.'*

I went. It was just the challenge and change I needed. I saw customers in Sweden, Denmark and Norway. Being British put me on cloud seven. I was welcomed, wined and dined. Every time I ate in a restaurant someone would pick up the bill. My hand was shaken and back patted so many times, everywhere. I lost count of the number of times I had to toast Churchill, the Royal Navy, the Royal Air Force and I forget what else. Peisal was right. The buyers did write out their orders and I phoned them back to Peisal twice a week. The mounting quantities gave me doubts. Peisal told me not to worry but just to sell every inch I could. As an experience it was the highest of highs. When I returned home I went back to staying in Amhurst Road. Peisal sent me a very handsome commission cheque. I moved into a cheerless flat off Haverstock Hill and later, when in Hackney, I always detoured so as not to pass the house.

And that wonderful chinoiserie furniture set? When I got back from Scandinavia it had, of course, gone. The Cohens and the Clarfelts were more upset than I was. They urged me to inform the police. I did not do so. About ten years later I saw the identical chinoiserie set in an up-market antique emporium off Queensway, identical down to the last details. It could well have been the same one. I looked at the price tag and felt sick. The sum asked could have kept me in luxury for many many years.

Back to the house. On the first floor, with its small barred window overlooking the back garden, was the toilet. It was adjacent to the door opening onto a flight of stone steps leading down into the garden. It was a route for getting in and out of the house unseen. If someone shot the inside bolt on the door then a clamber up the brick wall dividing the two gardens followed by a perilous climb up 12 feet of drainpipe onto a zinc-covered water tank platform was required. They built well in those days. That drainpipe had constant traffic and not a single bracket holding it to the wall ever loosened.

On that same floor the entrance hall to the front street door was wide. From it a short flight of stairs led up to the bathroom which was situated right above the toilet. Hot water came from an Ascot water heater. When the hot water taps were turned on the pilot light inside it flared up and ignited a ring of jets which whooshed into flame with an explosion that stopped the heart. Murphy's Law applied to that bathroom. It was the coldest room in the house and the two large sash windows askew in their frames allowed batteries of cold air jets to sweep in. Stepping out of a warm bath in winter meant goosefleshing all over immediately. Bathing was quick in, quick out, quickly grab a towel and even more quickly pull on clothing.

Twelve stairs up from the bathroom was my sisters' bedroom. It overlooked the back garden. From under their window sill a tiled roof about ten feet wide sloped down to cover the garden side of my parents' bedroom. The roof had a deep gutter. Quite often a tennis or sorbo or even a cricket ball would lodge in this gutter. To retrieve it I, being the youngest and lightest, would climb out onto the sloping roof holding the end of a belt. A brother would hold the other end while I slithered down to retrieve the ball. Games had to go on. The one time I let go of the belt was when neighbour Bessie Cohen came out and saw me on the edge of the roof. She was a hysterical girl at the best of times who irritated her neighbours by singing opera for long spells at full-belt soprano. At the sight of me she screamed, and screamed. She unnerved me. I

11

lost grip on the belt, slid down the tiles and fell over the edge, dangling, with both hands clutching the gutter. I faced a drop either onto Mum's favourite geranium bed or onto the adjacent concrete strip outside the kitchen window. 'Hang on!' screamed Bessie, 'Hang on. I'll phone the Fire Brigade.' 'No, Bessie,' yelled Sam. He dashed down to stop her. The gutter was firm. I managed to haul myself back onto the roof, spreadeagling myself along it with right foot and right hand jammed into the gutter for support. Mick appeared and threw me a length of rope. I grabbed it, flipped the ball into the garden and was hauled back. The game carried on. Phil Cohen emerged from his medical studies, grinning. He told us 'Bessie's flat on her back on a sofa frantically sniffing smelling salts.'

The two front rooms on this floor were occupied by tenants, a Mr and Mrs Stark, a quiet, neatly dressed childless couple who were never any trouble. He had survived the trenches in the First World War. I hated shaking hands with him because the two middle fingers of his right hand were down to stumps and the contact gave me goosepimples. Every morning he would creep downstairs in his dark three-piece single-breasted suit with starched detachable white collar and subdued tie and return at six o'clock to tread quietly up to his rooms, wishing a pleasant good evening to anyone he encountered. They never went out in the evenings and Mrs Stark only went out to go shopping. We all respected their privacy and as we grew older and came home later we took off our shoes before reaching their landing.

Mr Stark repaired clocks and watches. In the summer Mum would invite them to come down and sit in the garden. They never did. Possibly because I was the youngest the Starks used to invite me into their flat. The few times I went in there Mrs Stark would offer me an apple saying how healthy it was to eat. I always declined and Mr Stark would suggest that perhaps I would prefer an orange. I would decline again, and likewise to the offer of a drink. It was completely irrational but

I was slightly afraid of them. I would slide out hearing them say that I was always welcome. Later, I felt very ashamed of what must have been my churlish behaviour towards such a kindly couple.

We four boys slept in the two rooms on the next floor. Sam and Mick shared the street-side room. Aubrey and I slept in the back. Up above was Mary's domain.

Mornings were always a scramble to use the bathroom and toilets. To ease pressure Aubrey and I used the outside toilet, situated under the stone staircase leading from the first floor down to the garden. In summer, its thick plaster kept it cool. In winter, it was an ice box. It sustained an active population of large fearless spiders. They and the cold hastened our functions. We kept a small billet of wood to hand. While sitting I banged it against the walls and floor but was too squeamish to kill them. Aubrey was less so and the squashed remains of numerous spiders made me shudder.

Only Sam never participated in the morning rush. He never got out of bed before ten o'clock and often rose much later. Mum, worried, asked Dr Sachs what was wrong with him. Dr Sachs always pandered to Mum. He gave Sam a cursory going-over and said reassuringly 'There is nothing to worry about, Mrs Beckman. He suffers from a very common illness. Its symptoms are going to bed very late and getting up too late. Otherwise he is a very strong and healthy young man.'

There was never anyone so laid back as Sam. Nothing could faze him, hurry him or jolt him out of his deep trench of placidity. Dad's volubility when Sam joined his business in the early 1930s and invariably got in well after Dad had opened the shop erupted frequently into rows at home. The shouting by Dad at Sam so upset Mum, Mary and the girls that they would disappear upstairs. There were two reasons for Dad's anger. One was disappointment that Sam had not done better scholastically, for he was no fool. As Rose told him, what is the point in having a good brain if you are too lazy to use it. Also, Dad was not too happy at a struggling business having to support two wages instead of one. Dad was a wholesale and cut length textile merchant in New Road in the East End. During the recessional 1930s Dad was always struggling to keep his head above water like so many other small businesses.

Dad was well-liked, respected and a soft touch for a hard luck story. He never pressed hard for debts even when he needed the payments to pay his own suppliers. He was, of course, an easy victim for a species of crook known as the long-firmer. Mr Long-firmer was a crook who knew exactly how to operate on the right side of the law. He was well-dressed, well-spoken, plausible and certainly the sort of man anyone would buy a second-hand car from. He was pitiless, utterly ruthless and totally geared to making easy money from the honest and the gullible.

He would open a shop or warehouse, move in with the minimum of expenditure on fitting it out, install a phone, print the necessary calling cards and stationery and he was in business. He would do the rounds of buying small quantities from various suppliers. He would pay these early invoices on time, even before time, financing initial payment with money made from previous operations. As confidence in him grew his suppliers would give him larger amounts and more time to pay their invoices. Long-firmer played them with all the skill of an experienced angler landing a salmon. His reputation would grow and he would increase the number of his suppliers.

When he decided that his stocks were large enough to enable him to sell them off and make a killing he moved fast. He knew exactly who would buy his stock at bargain prices and would pay cash and ask no questions. He issued no invoices. Somehow his account books would disappear before the end. The decision to move on made, he indulged in a frenzy of quick selling, always for cash. He still took in goods and sold them as well. He took more time to pay. The few creditors who pressed for money would be fobbed off with promises, post-dated cheques and plausible mendacity. And then came the day when a creditor would go round to demand his money and encounter locked doors. He would peer through the windows and see an emptied warehouse and he would know that Mr Long-firmer had flown with his loot. All in cash. Those who complained to the police would be told that it was a civil action and it was not a criminal matter.

Long-firmers could never be touched. They operated through the protection of a limited liability company which meant that only the company's assets, if any, could be seized. His own personal possessions were untouchable. He never signed personal guarantees, nor ran foul of bank charges on his assets. Their depradations sank many a small struggling business.

Mick entered the business in the mid-1930s. Unlike Dad and Sam, Mick was hewn from meaner tougher material. He quickly saw the lie of the land. Supported by Rose, who kept the books and typed and would get quite upset at the bad debts Dad incurred solely through misplaced trust, Mick refused credit to those he mistrusted, demanded payment against pro-forma invoices from others and issued writs to very reluctant payers. Some were Dad's friends and members of Dad's synagogue. This was most embarrassing and pushed Dad into bitter quarrels with Mick. Mick would be unbudgeable. Bad debts diminished. Payments quickened. Money flowed in better and Mum could shop with more in her purse. Between Sam's late rising and indolent interest in the firm and Mick's toughness Dad did not have a happy time.

School, exams, sport, career; all these waned in interest for me during the 1930s. I became avid and intrigued by all the news and happenings and politics of the times. With Nazi Germany rampant in Europe, Italy waging modern warfare against bows and arrows in Abyssinia and the arrival of Jewish refugees every week I found schoolwork becoming a little irrelevant. This showed in reproving comments in my school reports.

And in Hackney in the 1930s one encountered British fascists every day and everywhere, arrogant in the certainty that their day in the saddle was coming. Around the mid-1930s there were two antagonistic fascist parties in Hackney; Mosley's British Union of Fascists and Arnold Leese's Imperial Fascist League. Leese was the most rabid anti-semite. He sneered at Mosley's softness, dubbing him the 'Kosher Fascist'. Their supporters were antagonistic and even fought among themselves. Nevertheless, it ill behove Jews to be careless and off guard if they went out after dark.

Incidents proliferated, usually concerning Jews being beaten up by roaming gangs of both fascist parties. Retaliation was rare. Yet, it did happen. One afternoon a Jewish man, walking past the IFL headquarters in Bodney Road, was set upon and badly hurt by a group who rushed out of the building when they saw him walking past. A Jewish girl happened to witness it. After she phoned for an ambulance and helped the man she rushed home and told her family about it. Their home was in Amhurst Road. She had four brothers, noted for their athleticism in various sports which included wrestling and boxing. The four boys picked up cricket bats and indian clubs and stormed into the IFL headquarters. By then, the building had emptied but they found three fascists. They tore into them with a will. Three more casualties went to the local hospital. Then, they smashed up everything in sight. No police action was taken. The IFL moved their headquarters to Balls Pond Road near the headquarters of their hated BUF.

It was the Spanish Civil War that really added bite to the Hackney political scene. Overnight there was a perceptible increase in anger between fascists and anti-fascists and acute polarisation. You either supported Franco or the Republicans. There could be no neutrals. There was a proliferation of marches and meetings supporting one side or the other. When two opposing sides clashed, usually communists and fascists, very quickly cat-calling gave way to scuffling which in turn gave way to bitter no-quarter fighting. There were reports of young Jews acting as decoys and leading fascist gangs into communist ambushes. There were reports of coshes, knuckledusters, razor blades stitched into peaks of caps and steel bootcaps being used. Certainly, some were severely hurt.

Our heroes without doubt were the volunteers who sloped off to fight against Franco. A boy in The Grocers, my secondary school, named Sherman, was very politically motivated. He was in the Upper VI, heading for university. His father was an immigrant from Lithuania and owned a shop in Stoke Newington High Street. One morning Sherman did not come to school, nor the next, nor the next. The fourth day of his absence we were riveted by the sight of Sherman's father coming to school accompanied by a police sergeant. They saw the headmaster. Without saying a word to anyone Sherman had just disappeared. One week after his disappearance his parents received a postcard. It had been sent from Paris. It said 'By the time you get this I shall be with the International Brigade to fight for Republican Spain. Love.' He joined the Clement Attlee Battalion, composed entirely of British volunteers.

To his schoolmates he became the object of envy and admiration. He had left humdrum school life for a great adventure. At a battle by the Guadalaraja he was hit by a bullet. It shattered his right knee cap. For several hours he had lain in agony in cold mud being soaked by heavy rain. They found him, operated on him and entrained him to Perpignan, whence he made his way home. He could never bend his right leg and walked with the aid of a stick. He never returned to school. His parents were distraught at his handicap but may have blessed it when the Second World War broke out.

I recollect three others who went from Hackney. One worked as an apprentice in Schlagman's butcher shop in Downs Park Road. No one knew what happened to him. He never returned to Downs Park Road. That was the form; the disappearance and then the postcard from Paris.

In the main boys at school kept their political views for the outside world. But once at The Grocers a large boy named Catkin broke this unwritten code. He brazenly sported the fascist lightning flash badge in his lapel. His bravura attracted lightning. One dark winter's evening Catkin was beaten up on his way home from school. His indignant father turned to see the headmaster and he named two Jewish boys whom his son said had been guilty of the assault. They denied it, saying they had gone straight from school to the Hackney Library in Mare Street to do their homework. They mentioned other boys who had been there. The other boys, not all Jewish, confirmed this. No action was taken. Several days later Catkin opened his school desk and found his badge. It had been bent and the back pin was snapped off. He never wore it again at school although he was seen in full fascist regalia at outdoor meetings.

At the age of six, one fraught morning, I had breakfast early and was then subjected to a detailed scrutiny by Rose and Mary. My black shoes shone with polish and spit. Mary massaged invisible wrinkles out of my grey woollen stockings cuffed down below my knees. My grey flannel shorts had been ironed into razor-edged creases and Aubrey's hand-me-down grey jersey had been washed and neatly darned. It also itched the underside of my chin.

'Come on,' said Rose firmly. She took my hand and led me out to attend my first day at school, Sigdon Road Elementary. Leaving the house and turning right we encountered Mrs Cohen sweeping her front garden path. Mrs Cohen was a frail, kindly mousy woman and, like Mum, she was always working. She and her husband both came from Poland. He owned a small factory off Queensbridge Road where he made up-market furniture. He was a cabinet-maker. Call him a furniture manufacturer and he would reply angrily that he

18

was a craftsman, not a chopper. He was a tall broad powerful man, exciteable, impetuous and even bellicose. He feared no man, did Isaac Cohen. He adored his petite wife.

His great passion was his wireless. He perched it on a wooden stand he had made and stood it by his kitchen window. Home from work he would spend hours twiddling the knobs and getting Luxembourg, Berlin, Amsterdam and Paris and many stations in between. When he trawled a prize like Moscow or Mussolini speaking he would shout with delight and declare 'You see. I've got all the world in that little box.'

Almost opposite our house was a small synagogue. Roving blackshirts sometimes amused themselves by pulling down the notice board outside it and painting PJ on its brick walls. The occasional stone would break a window. One evening seven congregants were having a committee meeting inside, Mr Cohen among them. A group of blackshirts arrived and started to pull down the outside sign and notice board.

'The momserim (bastards),' yelled Mr Cohen. He rushed from the meeting and charged down the outside steps with all the speed and menace of a roused rhinoceros. He caught a startled young fascist and with one punch he felled him. He picked him up, shook him violently and hurled him to the ground again. He put his foot on the supine youth's chest just as a police car turned up.

A police sergeant jumped from the car and said to Mr Cohen, 'We had a phone call that you were being attacked. Do you need any help . . .?'

'Help?' interrupted the irate Mr Cohen 'Help? We don't need help. This little swine needs help . . . '

The sergeant took in the pulled down sign and notice board. He pulled the fascist to his feet and told him to bugger off. He eyed the muscled shoulders and bristling mien of Mr Cohen and said 'Well, sir, if you ever need our help, which I doubt, do call us . . . '

Chapter Two

The Cohens had three children, Phil, Bessie and Harry, born in that order. Phil kept very much to himself. I recollect him in crowded rooms stuck into a book in a deep armchair, completely ignoring the tumult around him. In 1939 he qualified as a doctor and volunteered for the army. In due course he made captain in the RAMC and served in field stations during the fighting in Burma. He was transferred from the 'Forgotten Army', as the 14th Army troops in Burma referred to themselves, to hospitals in India. Back home he married a very attractive girl. Her father was a wealthy manufacturer of ladies' coats and he set up Phil in a surgery in Hampstead Garden Suburb. He developed a deserved reputation as the doctor to go to. He had two sons.

Bessie was plain, but compensated with shapely long legs and an hour glass figure that made boys overlook her face. Her penchant for singing operatic arias at full lung power every morning was the one thing that roused Sam from his deep slumbers. She was a good-natured likeable girl. Everyone was fond of her, even Sam, although when her morning screeches awakened him he was known to have shouted out of a window overlooking the back garden 'I'd pay someone to cut that bloody girl's vocal chords.'

Harry was just under two years older than I was. We were friends of a sort for two reasons; propinquity and because he had no other friends. He was a loner, a brooding strong boy with a sense of menace about him. When we shook hands he always gripped hard enough to cause gasps of pain. He was basically very shy and tended to seek me out, no problem as there was a gap in the brick wall between our gardens down to earth level. No one gave a thought to closing it.

A long brick wall 12 feet high divided the back gardens in our section of houses from the spacious builder's yard behind. During the days tennis and cricket balls would go over this high back wall and after dark our forays into adventureland began. There were occasions when up to a dozen small boys all along that wall would be cautiously slithering over it into that exciting jungle of everything that a successful firm of builders used; stacks of timbers and planks, drains of all widths and sizes, piles of porcelain toilets and enamelled tin baths and quantities of all that went into buildings. Our hearts pounded as we crouched over shaded torches and sought the missing balls.

The builder had four sturdy sons so we always posted a look-out half-way up the sycamore at the back of our garden. He was a great mimic of bird-songs. From his vantage point he could see right into the builder's house. If he saw him or one of his sons emerging into the yard he would imitate a wood-pigeon. The more easily-frightened boys would scuttle back along pre-selected routes over the wall to safety. Others would crouch as still as threatened badgers in their hidey-holes, ears, strained, and breaths, held. I crawled under a sturdy wooden batten supporting rolls of tarpaulin. It was a reversal of big game hunting. We were the quarry.

The yard was also home for a plethora of feral cats, living on what they scrounged and caught. Fledglings falling from their nests had no chance. Rats and mice had a hard time. During mating season the cats fought and howled the nights away. The disturbed Sam compared them morosely to a bunch of Bessie Cohens.

One afternoon I was with Harry at the back of his garden.

One of the two dustbins had its lid off. Harry raised his hand and hissed 'Shush.' He had spotted a cat inside it, eating the throw-away food. He crept forward silently, picked up the lid and slammed it down on top of the dustbin. 'Don't do that' I protested. 'Take it off.' 'I'll teach it a lesson,' smirked Harry. He whipped off the lid with his left hand and with his right threw a half brick at the cat. It hit the cat's head. It uttered one final howling shriek that froze my blood. It died instantly. It was the first time I had witnessed a death and the first time I had ever suffered a surge of physical sickness. I screamed at Harry. Even he was shaken. He slammed the lid back onto the dustbin and muttered 'I didn't mean to kill it.' 'That's why you threw the brick so hard,' I said, still shocked. He took my arm. I knocked his hand away as I walked back to the gap in the wall. His composure cracked. He pleaded 'What shall I do? I can't leave it for the dustmen to see.' 'Bury the bloody thing,' I suggested. I was so affected that I could only mangle my favourite supper of boiled viennas, chips and peas. Mary wondered what ailed me. I did not tell her, nor anyone. Harry buried the cat in a deep hole by the May tree close to the dustbins. Perversely, what he termed my brainwave raised my stock with him tremendously. After that incident our friendship cooled. We had nothing in common to bind it. Later, he qualified as a dental surgeon and served overseas with the Royal Army Dental Corps.

Onwards to my first day at school. Rose prised us away from Mrs Cohen. We walked round the Mitford Tavern, later a favourite pub for the fascists, into Sandringham Road, past the two short rows of shops that we knew so well. There was Maisie's delicatessen. He was a short pot-bellied man with a trimmed pointed greying beard and with small button eyes lurking behind rimless spectacles. He was devout and always wore his *yarmulka* (skull cap). His wife and daughter helped him in the shop. They were timid background women who retired from the scene when Maisie, who revelled in argument, held forth trenchantly on topics of the day, those he thought he knew about and those he knew nothing about. But his shop was a paradise of rich savoury smells, a feast in themselves. There were barrels of pickled herrings, anchovies in brine, roll-mops and smoked mackerels, bucklings and other fish. There were new green and sweet and sour pickled cucumbers, garlic wursts, cold meats which included succulent wodges of salt beef. There were cream cheeses, sour cream, smetana and trays of barley, chick peas, cloves, bay leaves and beans of every sort. Everything to titillate a Jewish stomach was there. It was a busy shop.

Opposite was Debbie's, run by Debbie Samuels, a kind chatty sunny woman. Whenever I went in there Debbie would dive her hand into a large tin under the counter and give me a handful of broken biscuits. She did this to all the other small boys who shopped there. She never failed and we all suspected that she broke up good biscuits to keep that tin filled. If customers lacked money to pay for purchases Debbie would tell them to take what they wanted, saying: 'If you need it, you need it. You can pay me later, when you can.'

She never made a note of the debt. I never heard of anyone letting her down. Her husband died in the early 1950s. Debbie ran the shop into the late 1970s. She carried on because she was lonely and liked to meet and talk with people. By the late 1960s the shop had become too much for her. She did not care for the new customers. Young unemployed blacks would come into her shop several-handed, take things without paying and scatter out of the shop. They never harmed nor menaced her but she found it ugly and upsetting. One day I found the shop closed. The Turkish Cypriot cleaners next door told me that she had gone. They did not know where.

Next to Debbie's was a hardware shop and next to that a trousers workshop where Morry Grossman and his son Jack manufactured men's trousers. Morry was a skeletal, careworn well-read socialist who chain-smoked and complained bitterly that all his life he had worked hard to get nowhere. His hands shook so uncontrollably that when he wielded a large pair of razor-sharp shears everyone gave him a wide berth. In the 1960s my company bought his small business. Morry and Jack stayed with it. Morry continued to live on cigarettes and strong tea and chain-smoked until his death from cancer in the early 1970s.

Next to Grossman's workshop were the Robinsons, news-agents, tobacconists and confectioners. Boys from local schools packed their shop every lunchtime. Mrs Robinson was a plump rosy-cheeked woman with exhausted mien. Greying hair pulled tightly into a bun at the nape of her neck framed her round face. She always complained smilingly that she needed ten pairs of hands to cope. Her husband was as taciturn as his wife was loquacious. He had a surprisingly craggy face and wore a fresh brown cotton coat every day. It was said that Mr Robinson had been badly wounded going over the top of the first day of the Battle of the Somme. It was a rowdy good-humoured shop as we drove them mad with our urgent demands for gobstoppers, sherbert balls, liquorice allsorts, tiger nuts, brandy balls, fruit drops and the multitude of confection kept in rows of airtight jars on shelves running the length of the wall behind the counter.

My favourite shop was the retail dairy on the other side of the road, adjacent to Maisie's. It was run by two ash-blonde Welsh sisters, spinsters, who spoke with that delightful Welsh lilt. Mum insisted that I bought butter and cheese there because it was so much fresher than anywhere else. The shop was always scrubbed spotless and fragrant with aromas from the purest of food products. The butter was a large cube on a white marble surface. When I ordered a pound weight one of the sisters would carve it out with two wooden paddles, pat it into a perfect rectangular shape and, when they weighed it, it was always bang on target, needing no addition or taking away.

Rose walked me to the corner to turn into Wayland Avenue

and we were met by Mr Kramer, our neighbourhood milk-man. His dairy was on the corner of Wayland Avenue. Behind it was a large yard with a shed for his horse. Once a day a keen gardening couple called in to take the horse's manure. That and the bales of hay gave off a country smell. Mr Kramer was a tall beanpole of a man, over six feet. He always wore a dark single-breasted suit with a very short jacket which in a later fashion period would have been called a bum-freezer. His trousers were tight and ended two inches above his ankles. A bowler hat, a size too small, perched on his head horizontally to the ground.

He was a stalwart of the Dalston Talmud Torah, that small synagogue in Amhurst Road. One sensational evening the elders of that synagogue fell out and Dad and his cronies changed allegiance to Stoke Newington synagogue. It was quite dramatic, the equivalent of an Irish night out without the Guinness. Synagogue politics was a sport where hard-working worried men could let off steam. It was said that Mr Kramer performed stalwartly trying to make the peace between the two sides. As everyone else present enjoyed the war, he failed.

He was a familiar and popular figure in the streets of Hackney as he perched on the driving seat of his two-wheeled cart, smoking his pipe, bowler hat on head, and quartered the areas with his customers. Four large churns were battened onto his cart and contained milk fresh from the farm. He had a resonant far-reaching call and when he turned into our road the women would emerge with bowls and jugs. Kramer had two measures, a pint and a half-pint jug for pouring. He was a liked man and many invited him in for coffee or tea. He always declined gratefully. But one sultry July morning he succumbed to Mrs Galinsky's offer of cold home-made lemonade. As he sat in her lounge sipping it and talking, a neighbour knocked at the door and called out frantically 'Mr Kramer. You must come quickly.'

Unhurriedly, as was his way, he strode out into the street

25

and saw a row of cats blissfully lapping at the milk spilling from his cart into the gutter. It was a school holiday. Groups of giggling boys were watching the happy cats. No one ever owned up to having turned on the spigot but as Mr Kramer said philosophically as he turned it off 'Well, a *mitzvah* is still a *mitzvah* (good deed) even if it only benefits cats.'

He had two pretty daughters. When I innocently wondered why boys seemed to hang around that corner Sam said drily 'They're not after milk, that's for sure.'

Mr Kramer patted me on the head for luck and Rose led me up Wayland Avenue, a short stretch lined by nondescript terraced houses. At its end was a jam factory which exuded a sickly smell that pervaded everywhere. Before we reached it we turned left into Sigdon Road and about 100 yards down on the right I saw the red-bricked institutional box of a building that was Sigdon Road Elementary School. It stood four storeys high. Opposite, the other side of Dalston Lane, was Hackney Downs station, a London and North-Eastern Railway station.

I slowed down. Rose pulled me through the tall wrought-iron gates into a concrete playground filled with a noisy maelstrom of noisy, shouting, running scuffling boys. The caretaker closed the gates at nine o'clock, opened them for the lunch hour's break, closed them at two o'clock and opened them again at four. This made playing truant difficult but boys could and did climb like monkeys. I expressed a strong desire to go home. Rose gave me a hug and a kiss on my cheek and handed me over to a young man, a new teacher, who joked that we were both in the same boat.

The entire flat roof of the school was a playground. We spilled onto it during the 20-minute morning break. It was surrounded by a ten-foot high wall. That first morning break my cap was snatched from my head and thrown over that wall. I had to run down the concrete staircases to retrieve it. Other new boys suffered the same fate. We gave one another rueful looks as we passed and re-passed on the staircases. It happened to me once more, after which I stuffed the cap underneath my jersey.

Looking back it was amazing how ingenious boys were at devising simple games from thin air, like throwing six stones into the air and catching as many as possible before they hit the ground and trying to hit a running, weaving ducking boy with a tennis ball. Top-spinning was widespread. The tops were wooden and pear-shaped, with a metal point protruding from the sharp end. Screw-like threading was cut into the wood from top to bottom. You wound the requisite length of twine tightly round into the entire threading, looped the end of it over your index finger for grip and then hurled the top at the ground. This unwound the twine and spun the top. At the very last moment you jerked your arm sharply upwards and, as the top parted from the twine, it spun on its metal point with a gratifying humming. Where aficionados gathered to see who could spin their tops the longest, farthings and half-pennies changed hands in surreptitious bets.

But the most popular of all such sports was played with glarneys. Glarneys were solid glass spheres veined with multi-coloured patterns like exotic paperweights. They could be bought in different sizes. The larger they were the more they cost. Sizes ranged from the diameter of a cricket ball down to the throwing glarneys which were half an inch in diameter. The largest cost four pence, two weeks' pocket money for me, down to one halfpenny for six of the smallest throwing glarneys.

During breaks boys with the large prize glarneys set up shop in the playground. They sat on the ground, their legs wide apart and the prize between their feet. From an agreed distance the throwers would roll their small glarneys at it. If they hit the prize it became theirs. The game had unwritten codes of conduct. For example, the winner of a prize was honour bound to set up shop to give the erstwhile owner a chance to win it back.

Glarneys had its wrinkles. Boys would set up their prize glarneys on a pitch where the surface was roughened. Throwers would scrutinise the lie of the land as carefully as a championship golfer examines a putting green. A constant hazard were predatory gangs, usually three in number, who strove to win glarneys by intimidation and brute strength. They were very effective.

One morning I saw such a beautiful glarney in Robinsons' I had to buy it. It cost threepence. Came the morning break I set up stall, intrigued to see how many small glarneys came my way. I kept an eye out for the one boy who was notoriously deadly of aim. His accuracy was incredible. He won many a prize with his first shot. Boys, seeing him appear, would pick up their prize glarneys and wait until he had passed by.

I set up shop near a wall and waited for customers. I had collected three small glarneys when I became aware of three boys older and burlier than me standing behind. One grabbed my hair and at the same time another snatched my prize. I saw red and grabbed the hand clutching my prize. A clenched bony fist banged down on the top of my head and three evil faces hissed at me what they would do to me if I reported the incident. The Mafia trio strolled away. Other boys rushed over to tell me what the terrible three had done to other boys. Every break two masters walked around that upper playground to keep an eye on things. They blind-eyed the occasional fight. Unless a boy was in danger of being thrown over the wall to certain death they let nothing interfere with their cosy chat. I was so indignant I was going over to speak to them but was stopped by other boys with cooler heads. I never bought another prize glarney. At least, I could eat chocolate.

When I arrived home for lunch, tearful at my humiliating loss, cousin Nat was there. He was some ten years older than I was but he was a most powerful young man. He boxed. He worked out on wrestling mats and heaved heavy bolts of

28

fabric about in his father's warehouse. He popped me onto a chair and asked what had happened. I told him.

'Right.' He lifted my chin so that I had to stare into his face. 'It's a hard world and being Jewish makes it that much harder. You've got to make yourself so able to fight that you'll never fear a one to one confrontation. Not with anyone.'

He took the pains to come over and teach me to fight. He taught me to stand sideways on, to present a smaller target, to punch my weight and to increase the speed of my punching. Wrestling matches with my brothers made me realise that I was physically strong. Nat added technique and strove to imbue me with a killer instinct, such as finding an opponent's weak spot and going for it hell-for-leather. Within the year the training paid off. Anti-semitism before the advent of Mosley and his fascists in the 1930s was no real problem in Hackney. There were those who disliked Jews and derived their kicks from passing insulting personal remarks. A large and older boy made me his target. Because I turned a deaf ear to his snide remarks he persisted and persisted in his verbal molestation. One dull December evening I followed him as we left school and in an alleyway leading from Amhurst Road into Hackney Downs I jumped him. I gave him a fair beating. Never again was I physically or verbally molested at Sigdon Road Elementary School.

Thus, I learned one of life's lessons. It may be better to be respected than liked. But, it is far more potent to be feared.

Chapter Three

My time at Sigdon Road Elementary passed in a blur. Teachers were Gods, to be obeyed and heeded. Quite a number of them had survived the war but, with one exception, never spoke about their service experiences. This jovial extrovert taught geography. At whim he would stop a lesson and regale his class with his experiences in Mesopotamia. The phrase 'When I was in Mesopotamia . . .' became a hallowed school catchphrase. To us boys, of course, the World War was just history.

Our masters all wore dark suits, white shirts and quiet ties. They were beardless and with hair trimmed to short back and sides. Their shoes gleamed. They placed great emphasis on personal appearance. Boys who came to school looking scruffy would be highlighted in trenchant terms. The culprits would appear the following day with blemishes rectified. There was no egalitarian 'let us be friends' nonsense. Discipline was strict, but fair. We all knew where we stood and because of this felt secure and happy. They called us by our surnames. 'Adams. Beckman. Cohen. Jenkins. Roberts. Smith . . . ' To which roll call we would shoot up our hands and reply smartly 'Sir. Sir. Sir. Sir. Sir. Sir.'

I cannot recall an Asian or black pupil. The five per cent ethnic mix were all Jewish, the progeny of East European immigrants. Although we were British-born we were the aliens, a status imposed upon us by our religion. Our rigidly orthodox fathers forced their beliefs onto us by one-sided debate aided sometimes by the force of a powerful right arm. Religion was never up for debate. It was there to be followed. That was that.

The school allowed Jewish boys to take days off from school for all the High Holidays. This was always a matter of envy by the Christian boys who had to attend school while we were absent. Compounding this was the fact that Jewish boys did win a disproportionately high number of scholarships to good secondary and grammar schools. Little did our Christian schoolmates know about the pressures many of us were under from fathers paranoid that we did well.

No master really stood out. Looking back I am sure it was because they were all of a uniformly high standard. We had little homework but when in class we really had to knuckle down, pay attention and learn. Thus, we all learned the basics in the main subjects quite early. When the teachers swept into the classrooms we stood and chorused respectfully 'Good morning, sir' or 'Good afternoon, sir' and then it was straight into the lessons.

Every classroom had an enormous rectangular blackboard behind the master's desk. The blackboard had a gulley along its bottom which held chalks and small hooks for dusters. Some teachers really made the chalk fly as they illustrated and diagrammed. As they chalked, they explained, working their way across the blackboard to the other side. When they reached it they would vigorously rub out all their work with a duster and start anew. Those blackboard expositions certainly concentrated our minds. We learned to absorb knowledge before it was wiped out.

This pressure to make us learn quickly did eliminate class-room trouble. Boys playing up were unpopular with other boys and those who lost the threads of the lesson just fidgeted fractiously. But, that was all. After school classmates who did not understand the lessons battened onto those who did. We took helping one another for granted.

31

Punishment for disruption of a lesson fell into three distinct stages. The first time an offender would be made to stand with his face towards the wall. The second time he would be made to stand outside the classroom. If he misbehaved a third time he would be sent to the headmaster with a note. This usually merited six whacks with a cane across his backside or, more painful, across the palm of his hand. Seldom did an offender disrupt again.

The dreaded ultimate punishment was expulsion. I recall it happening on two occasions; once with a boy whose offence was never revealed but it was strongly rumoured that it concerned a girl from a local school. The other time two incorrigible bullies who had been in trouble before for way-laying smaller boys and taking their money were caught red-handed stealing from outerwear in the school cloakroom. Virtually the entire school watched their grim-looking fathers come into the school and leave with their very frightened sons.

During breaks I would join in one of the many games of football and cricket in the playgrounds. I took to the sports like a duck to water and was quickly picked for the infant school's team. At that time brother Aubrey was in the senior school and played for the school teams in both games. My burning desire to play alongside him remained unfulfilled. When I played for the senior school XIs Aubrey had long since moved to Hackney Downs Secondary, The Grocers.

Lunch break lasted for one hour. As noon struck I was through the gates at a run and home within eight minutes. My omelette, chips and peas would be on the table waiting for me. As I ate I read those marvellous weekly boys' papers. They cost twopence each. There was the *Adventure*, the *Wizard*, the *Magnet*, which ran the Billy Bunter and Greyfriars School stories, the *Hotspur* and others. The stories were so well written that they must have been a definite factor in making us so literate at an early age. Cartoon comics did not exist.

Five of us each bought a different weekly so by swapping around we could each read five for the price of one. There were many heroes in those weeklies but my hero was a goal-keeper named Cast-iron Bill. He never let in a goal. Opposing teams always failed to put a penalty past him. Yet, there was one centre-forward who had never failed with a penalty. The meeting of these two was developed through several issues and we all acquired a tremendous thirst for the momentous confrontation to come. When the relevant issue came out I rushed into Robinson's to buy it and stood outside the shop devouring the story. Would Cast-iron Bill be beaten by the penalty king? He was not. No penalty was given, enabling the suspense to be sustained for many more issues. I felt cheated. In addition, I was scolded by Mary for getting home late and letting the lunch grow cold.

Dad's family. He had had three brothers. One left Poland and went straight to Palestine where he worked on pioneer, draining swamps and breaking up rocks to create soil. He was an uncle who for me may never have existed. Another was the father of the brilliant chartered accountant, Henry, who disappeared so mysteriously. The eldest, Abraham, I did meet from time to time. He settled into a large house with deep back and front gardens in Stamford Hill. Like Dad, he was very devout. Every morning he rushed to synagogue to don phylacteries and pray. Later, he would rush home from work and then to synagogue for afternoon and evening prayers. There were many like him. In the early days he and Dad were partners. They fell out and went their different ways, but remained on cordial terms socially.

Abraham was a textile merchant, more ruthless, less gullible and very much more successful than Dad. He was short, full bearded and not given to the volatile vulnerability that plagued his brother. He was cautious and shrewd and at family functions kept a low profile. Like Dad he never bothered to master English and when they met they spoke in Yiddish.

33

He had three sons, Barney, Sam and Nat, and four daughters, Milly, Rose, Freda and Jean. Jean married Ben Landau, a successful textile merchant. Ben was a short, Napoleonic dapper man with a deep resonant voice. He would have made an excellent town crier. It was his voice that gave him his one claim to fame. How it developed, no one knew. It was this.

After the Israelis won their War of Independence in 1948 guests at Jewish functions toasted the State of Israel in addition to the Loyal toast. There were many functions at that time with so many up and coming relations about but, somehow, it was Ben, always Ben, who proposed the toast to Israel. It came after the Loyal toast. It was Ben's big moment. He savoured every second leading up to it, refusing wine, dabbing his lips with his napkin and coughing gently to clear his throat. The moment would come when the red-coated Master-of-Ceremonies would bang the top table with his gavel and announce 'Pray silence, ladies and gentlemen, if you please, for Mr Ben Landau, who will propose the toast to the State of Israel and its President.'

Ben would rise slowly and look around the tables, very slowly. He would raise his glass dramatically high above his head with all the gravity of an athlete holding the Olympic torch aloft and he would demand in booming measured tones 'Ladies and Gentlemen (pause), would you please charge your glasses and rise (pause) and with me (long pause) toast the State of Israel and its President.'

It was said that Israel was created purely for Ben. Although Ben was a bit on the pompous side you could joke with him but never about his toasting. One cousin devised a comic sketch wherein the Presidents of Israel, at State functions in Tel Aviv, would rise and toast Ben Landau. It was hilarious. I doubt whether Ben ever knew about it.

Scandals those days were few and far between. They were kept away from young ears like mine for fear of contaminating them. It was Nat, a frequent visitor to our home, who opened my eyes. He was sitting down having tea and butter biscuits with Mum, talking conspiratorially, when he spotted me lurking and ordered me out of the kitchen. I went out, clumped heavily up the stairs and tip-toed down to listen by the ajar kitchen door. It was worth the risk.

Nat's sister Rose had married a layabout, named Bert. He gambled. He drank. Bert was that rare Jew who then frequented pubs. He was always short of money. He was one of life's non-copers. He often went home drunk and through stress caused by his own weaknesses he started to knock Rose about. It was his biggest mistake. Nat went round and knocked hell out of Bert. No one knows what was said and done but Bert vanished from the scene. Rose and her family were fully supported in every way by their family.

Barney was quiet and studious, bespectacled and with the curiosity of the very intelligent. He went to the University College of London. He became a rabbi and took up a post in South Africa. Returning after several years he qualified as a solicitor and went into practice. He married Hilda, a university graduate. They had three sons who all went to Oxford and qualified in law. In the 1980s Phillip, Norman and Brian were running a well-founded family practice in the West End.

Sam, the eldest, was the achiever. He had an ice cold brain and was ruthless with it. The 1930s saw London's Jewish community taking deep root as the oldest of the British-born generation pushed the frontiers of success far and wide. A. Beckman, Ltd., controlled and run by Sam, was one of the companies that led the pack. Nat was no fool, but he could be compassionate. This was a weakness in business which could cost money. It was a weakness that Sam kept a beady eye on.

Sam was in the vein of earlier merchant adventurers who initially went further and wider afield than their competitors and thus prospered. They went to Prato early, a well-spread sunburnt town in Tuscany, regarded as the largest producer of woollen fabrics of all types in the world. Prato is close enough to Florence to enable buyers to stay in Florence and enjoy its fabulous treasures. When cousin Sam imported the first consignments of goods they ran into problems. Standards of quality acceptable in the Italian market were regarded as sub-standard by the more sophisticated British market. Goods sold and delivered, were rejected and returned to A. Beckman's warehouse. Payment to Italy was withheld. For Sam it was, through no intention or making on his part, a no lose situation. The Pratesi manufacturers did not want the goods back. They would have to pay for the shipping and packing and then they would have to find new customers for them. A. Beckman would settle to keep them for a fraction of the original price, so low, that they could sell them as seconds and make a profit. Or, to African markets where the Prato standards were acceptable.

Along with other merchants and not only from Britain, A. Beckman kept buying from Prato, lodging complaint and getting their reductions. Even before the war A. Beckman grew so quickly that their dealings with Prato became less and less. But, memories linger.

When my brother Sam was demobilised he set up in business in the only thing he knew, textile merchanting. He went to buy in Prato. He could speak Italian, which went down well. Compatible with his nature he built up a reputation for straight dealing and fairness. He crossed the divide between customer and friend and several of his suppliers would invite him home for dinner. This was indeed, rare.

But the legacies of the 1930s lingered on. He encountered them, as I did when I went to buy fabrics in Prato in the early 1950s for our factory. Sam had succeeded in putting bitter memories to rest. On one occasion a local agent collected me from the Hotel Baglioni in Florence, drove me to Prato to a mill owned by a Signor Altossini. When he introduced me as 'Signor Beckman da Londra' the tall thin Altossini threw up his arms and literally spat on the floor. 'You mean Signor

Complaint' he said, 'I don't want to do business with him.' 'Why not?' exclaimed my agent, as if he did not know. An enthralling histrionic argument ensued, which both seemed to enjoy.

My agent used my obvious age to prove that I could not be Mr Complaint. He patted my shoulder, turned me around and I thought he was going to show Altossini my teeth. My agent praised my gentlemanly character to the skies. Altossini ordered espresso coffees and we all agreed what gentlemen we all were. For years I bought from Altossini. It was a pleasant relationship and when problems arose with faulty goods we settled without my partner and I taking the full advantage of the situation. Then, on a trip a few years later Altossini was no longer there. He had been sunk by a fatal combination of bad debts, high overheads, domestic crises and a sleeping partner who had been robbing the till.

Of those first cousins my thoughts always returned to Nat. He was the only one who called into our home in Hackney which he did quite often. He was an extremely warm person who felt for others, especially his close relations. He was intensely Jewish, quick to take offence. When first I, then Mick, then Sam and then Aubrey went off to war he was intensely proud of us and when one of us came home on leave he loved to wine and dine us in one of the several top restaurants that he frequented.

One evening he was dining with Mick who had just flown in from Newfoundland on a Hudson lend-lease plane. Mick was subdued. One of the planes he had left with had gone missing with its crew and in those vast arctic wastes that they were routed over going down meant death. Mick knew the crew. At the next table sat four young Guards officers. They had dined well and were talking loudly in uncontrolled vinous voices. They were the military equivalent of what were later termed Hooray-Henrys. They were discussing new intakes and one said that his unit had acquired a second Jew-boy, a

Glaswegian spiv. Whereupon another of the four brayed 'I'm damned if I want any shit-scared Jew-boys on my lot.'

His high voice carried far and wide. The uncomfortable frisson at surrounding tables was broken by Nat. He got up and walked slowly over to the officers' table. Sensing trouble they turned to face him. Nat grabbed the offender and pulled him to his feet. He grabbed him under the chin and lifted his face so that they stood eyeball to eyeball and he said 'Would you like to come outside with this shit-scared Jew-boy?'

Mick said he had never felt so embarrassed. The entire restaurant fell still, and watched. Waiters stopped serving. The officer was disadvantaged. He knew he could not engage in a brawl in uniform. More to the point, he knew a fight with the powerful bristling Nat would have been no contest. Nat let him go and returned to his table. The officers paid their bill and quickly left. The Greek owner of the restaurant came over with a bottle of wine. He put it on the table and said 'On the house, Mr Nat. You did right. You must be pleased.' 'Not really, Costas,' said Nat. 'Those four will soon be fighting the Nazis for you and me. What is it about them that has that mentality, to make them think that way.'

Costas, an ageing worldly Greek, replied sadly 'Every country has them . . . those who are born, excuse me, with the sun shining out of their arseholes who automatically think of themselves as top of the human pile.'

At Sigdon Road School our noses were kept pressed against the grindstone of learning. There were no such things as fun projects or field outings to take up valuable time. Everything, work, sport, carpentry had the edge of competitiveness. We were well taught. Take English, my favourite subject. We were force fed punctuation, figures of speech, sentence construction, grammar and parsing and how to knit masses of words into correct coherent language. Each week we had to write an essay or short story on a given topic. Two out of ten was poor; five, passable; seven, good. One day I wrote a story and was awarded nine out of ten. The teacher read it out to the class. They were unimpressed. My toes curled inside my shoes.

Haircuts were a mandatory fortnightly ritual. Short back and sides were *de riguer* for all boys. Many of us frequented the small cosy barber shop under the iron bridge at Hackney Downs station. The shop supported its owner and his two assistants. The owner was a small pinched-face man in a clean white coat who, when not working, plumped into a semi-armchair and devoured newspapers and magazines. He commented on the world's problems with such certainty that everyone deferred to him. It was less exhausting than arguing against his amazing self assurance. He and his two assistants were Jewish.

Every lunch hour boys from schools would occupy the three chairs and queue. The barbers worked with amazing speed. Scissors clacked away with the non-stop precision of pistons and the floor became carpeted with hair. I preferred Harry, a thick-set short man with thick fingers and a grip like Samson's. When he grabbed your head and swung it to the side it was like being swung by a vice. When he worked at top speed he could be a little careless, especially when the 'guvnor' vouchsafed views on yet another of the world's problems. At which Harry would turn his head and growl, 'You don't know what you're talking about.'

It was at this point that Harry would clip off flesh instead of hair. Boys would leave the shop clutching blood-stained swabs of cotton wool to their ears. Sometimes the shop resembled a medical station on the western front. Harry's guvnor would protest anguishedly 'Harry. For God's sake. You're giving haircuts not earcuts.'

Came the war, Harry volunteered and went into a county infantry regiment. He was wounded in Holland and invalided out. He took a job in a barber shop in Amhurst Road by Hackney station. He sported a glass eye and a deep angry scar running down his cheek and neck to disappear into his shirt collar. He had lost two fingers on his right hand. He worked more carefully. He never spoke about the war nor engaged in the political banter that he used to enjoy in the other shop.

The third barber in that station shop was elderly, worn down by the struggle to make a living and the indignity of having to make morning tea and sweep up. He never took part in the arguments between his boss and Harry except to mutter to the clients in his chair 'They think they know every-thing. Schmocks. And I've got to listen to their bloody non-sense all day long . . . .'

Amhurst Road in those days was a pleasing place to live in. The summers comprised long dry spells that kept us out all the time. I loved watching the council workmen macadamising the road surface, stage by stage. They boiled the pitch in a huge mobile cauldron set over a glowing charcoal furnace while the two horses pulling the wagon would stand munch-ing placidly from the feed bags slung over their heads. It was the smell of the boiling pitch, tangy and addictable, that I enjoyed. When the workmen had completed one section they moved leisurely into the next. There was so little traffic they seldom bothered to protect themselves with cones.

Another hot day I was in our back garden when I heard a tremendous metallic bang. I rushed into the street and saw a rare motor accident at the intersection with Downs Park Road. A car and a motor cycle had collided. Both had been travelling at speed. One, or both, had not slowed when they met at the crossroads. Householders were emerging cautiously fright-ened of what they would see. Twenty yards from the accident I was treading on glass. A group of people were bending over the motor cyclist. He was writhing and groaning. Gentle hands were trying to hold him down. His trousers were soaked in blood and there were blood smears all over the pavement and roadway. The car was jammed against the brick wall of a front garden. It was stoven in, its bonnet was concertinaed and all the glass had gone from its windscreen and windows. Its driver, a middle aged man, sat on the running board, head in hands. Blood seeped through his fingers. He was being attended by a man and woman but was paying no heed to what they said.

Police arrived, swiftly followed by an ambulance. The police shooed the spectators away. The ambulancemen stretchered the now quiescent motor cyclist into their vehicle. They took the motorist as well. A tow vehicle arrived and took away the car, now a total wreck. The pieces of motor bike were piled neatly against another front garden wall.

But, what to do with the thick smears of blood? Schlagman, our kosher butcher, a few yards along Downs Park Road, hurried to the scene with two buckets filled with sawdust. He carefully sprinkled it over the blood. He had to return with two more buckets to cover all traces. It was the first road accident I had seen. It was a bad one. Yet it affected me little.

Although first sight of the injured motor-cyclist had shocked me I was able after that to watch proceedings in a completely detached manner, unlike Harry's murder of the cat. Perhaps the difference was between an accident and wilful murder. I told Mary about the crash as I tucked into lunch, omitting no gory detail. 'Howie,' she snorted 'you're a callous one. How can you eat?'

'Easily. I'm hungry.'

Chapter Four

Mary gradually melded into our way of life. Yiddish tripped off her tongue in a Geordie accent with commendable accuracy. She developed an interest in everything Judaic, especially the koshering and cuisine, and kept asking questions some of which we could not answer. It was comical watching the bear-like Mr Cohen speak gently to Mary in Yiddish and correcting her mistakes.

In contrast, as Dad's sons pulled away from the tightly chafing bonds of Judaism at accelerating speed, as we grew up, his wounded rebuke that Mary was becoming a better Jew than his children filled us with an initial deep guilt that did fade with time.

Yet, his religion remained his shield against all outside worries and griefs. He achieved his greatest moments of serenity when he was in synagogue. Every Friday, well before sunset, he hurried home, bathed and put on his black jacket and grey-striped trousers. He would carefully lift his black top hat from its box and spend ten minutes lovingly brushing it clockwise until it gleamed. Then, when we were still very young, he would urge his four sons into donning their best attire. This was the cue for Mary to go into her persistent sheepdog act. She would come into bedrooms and hurl ties and shirts at us and harangue us mercilessly into getting ready and scurrying down to join Dad. Then, we would march off in a compact group to Stoke Newington synagogue.

Soon Dad was marching ahead, alone, and we boys were

trailing along behind, playing football with stones or discarded cigarette cartons, only pausing to exchange 'Good Sabbaths' with congregants we encountered. Inevitably, our line straggled and when we turned corners there was always one, usually Sam, who was out of sight. Dad would shake his fist with anger at us and call out 'No shame. No respect.'

He was so intensely Jewish that when I crossed my legs for comfort in the pew he would snap at me 'Goy. Uncross your legs. You're not in church.' Bored by the long service we stage whispered behind cupped hands, until quietened by a severe 'Shush' or a cuff about the head. Even though the synagogues had a healthy attendance those days virtually all of my generation found the service too long, too repetitive. Most irritating were the cantors who felt they could sing, and some could, and stretched out their warblings by going back over the same word or phrase several times. Complaints to Dad about all this went down like lead balloons. He would scoff 'It's been good enough for Jews for two thousand years and along come my clever sons and want to change it.'

Yet, while restless in synagogue on Friday nights, we always had the apogee of the week to look forward to. It was that wonderful binding traditional Friday night dinner where all the family were at one at the culinary highlight of the week. The napery would be starched stiff white. The cutlery would be polished so that each piece gleamed reflecting the eight lit candles, the centrepiece of the table. There was banter, good-humour, smiles and we felt closer as a family than at any other times. A typical Friday night repast started with chopped liver, followed by chicken soup with dumplings, roast chicken with baked potatoes, tzimmas and kasha, and a dessert of crisp chewy lokshen pudding. Large tumblers of lemon tea washed it all down, after which we all sang Grace After Meals with great gusto.

It was the slavering anticipation of congregants for that Friday night feast that catapulted Mr Maisie to fame. Hebrew

is a tongue-twisting language to pronounce. The amazing Mr
Maisie not only read it more quickly than anyone else but he
also managed to enunciate every syllable clearly. So, when
the authorised cantor stood down after the afternoon service
ended to allow a lay member to conduct the evening service, a
highly regarded honour for the one chosen, Maisie's considerable claque would call out 'We want Mr Maisie. Maisie.
Maisie.' This would arouse admonitory shushings from outraged elders. Through it all Maisie would sit with arms akimbo
gazing up at the women's gallery's stained glass windows.
Invariably, he was chosen. In a coax-me-a-great-deal mood he
would don his prayer shawl and climb onto the *bima*, whence
he would lead the charge. Irreverent bets were placed as to
whether he would finish the normal 30-minute service in ten
minutes, or less.

A look around the congregation, a shooting of his cuffs,
and then Maisie would be away with a rush. The congregants
would chase after him pell-mell with their responses. The
murmuration of frantically-turned prayer book pages signi-
fied that many were losing track. Some sat, when they should
have been standing and others stood when they should have
been sitting. Some threw in the towel and closed their books.
Others pretended to be able to follow the service but as they
never bothered to turn a page they fooled no one. Maisie, utterly
oblivious to the chaos he was creating, swayed backwards
and forwards over the lectern like a speeded up metronome.
When he finished on a high triumphal note the congregation
responded with a congratulatory heartfelt shout of '*Shakoiach*'.
The bright spark who bearded Maisie and bet him one pound
that he could not break five minutes received a dusty answer.
To the very devout, like Maisie, Judaism was never a subject
for levity.

When income is swallowed by the paying of necessities for
eight people there is very little left for fripperies. Mum and Dad
never went out for months on end. But, very very occasionally,

they visited the Yiddish theatre. There were two in London; the Grand Palais in Commercial Road and the Alexandra Theatre in Stoke Newington High Street.

One evening they took me to see a famous troupe at the Alexandra. The dialogue was in Yiddish. I could understand most of it. The play was a melodrama. It exaggerated emotions to the nth degree. Passion was scorching, and grief, with actresses hurling themselves distraught across tables, beds, any flat surface, was . . . grief. Having paid good money for tickets the mainly working and artisan audience was determined to enjoy itself. They lapped up every word. Nor did they hold back from shouting advice to the actors on stage. I recall a scene where an evil gangster in stove pipe hat, black cutaway jacket and thin wide moustachio, snarled at his victim.

'If you don't give me money, I shall shoot you.'

'I have so little,' pleaded the distressed woman 'and what little I have I need for my children. They are starving. My husband is ill and can't work . . . .'

'That, my dear,' sneered the villain, 'is your problem. Now, no more wasting of time. Give me the money or I'll shoot you.'

'No. No.' The overcome victim collapsed into a chair, hands pressed to her head, sobbing as explosively as a mortar attack. 'What will happen to my children?'

They will starve and die', laughed the villain as evilly as was possible. 'Now, you stupid woman, I'll have to shoot you . . .', saying which, the villain reached deeply into his jacket pocket, whereupon a man in the audience shouted out 'It's not there. It's in the pocket on the other side.'

The villain swung round and doffed his tall hat at the man who had shouted and said 'Thank you, my dear sir.' Then, he put his hand in the other pocket and pulled out the gun. At that moment the husband arrived with a policeman and they overpowered the villain.

Later, fierce argument raged from 'How did the spectator know which pocket the gun was in?' to 'Schmock of an actor.

Fancy not knowing where the gun was' to possibilities of sleight of hand or perhaps he carried a gun in each pocket.

Intervals at the Alexandra would see a mad stampede out of the theatre and into Murgraff's, a roomy kosher eaterie next door. It was presided over by Murgraff himself, a large man with an always flushed moon face and small blinking eyes defensively watching the world through large-lensed tortoise-shell rimmed spectacles. He wore a white linen trilby and a starched white coat with the letter 'M' embroidered in red on its breast pocket. From the height of a platform running behind the counter he lorded it over his domain with a benign harrassment. His despairing litany that he only had two hands was sometimes chorussed by amused customers.

Pleading patience from hungry Jews whose taste buds had been turned on by the aroma of delicious foods was indeed spitting against the wind. The white marble counter top was a visual delight with bowls of crisp cucumbers, new greens, gherkins, pickled onions, grated horseradish, coleslaw, grated celeriac and carrot salads, salted peanuts and roasted cashew nuts and condiments of every type.

The centrepiece, on its throne-like block of scrubbed wood, was a huge slab of freshly pickled salt beef from which Murgraff carved slices with amazing dexterity and speed. He passed the slices to two white-coated young female assistants on either side of him. Their reddened faces perspired with heat and exertion as, with intense concentration, they put the beef into rye bread slices, cut the sandwiches into quarters, wrapped them in greaseproof paper and handed them to the customer. The bird-like Mrs Murgraff manned the cash desk by the door.

As time passed customers at the end of the queue would start to fret at getting back to their seats late. They would become vociferously anxious. Somehow, Murgraff always managed to serve them all in time. When the actors returned to the stage they would confront a sea of contented faces munching into sandwiches and viennas. Many teeth crunching into many pickled cucumbers sounded like the magnification of death watch beetles at work on an ancient timbered house.

Now and again in the 1930s the posters outside the Alexandra would be defaced and the ubiquitous letters PJ with the fascist flash in between would be daubed on the theatre walls.

Murgraff's salt beef on rye was legendary. The meat was always moist and fresh. The portions were generous and two sandwiches followed by apple strudel and lemon tea made a most satisfying meal. Lunchtimes, his place was always full. His customers were a mix of doctors, accountants, solicitors, estate agents, manufacturers and merchants. One sweltering day he worked in a new short-sleeved shirt which he had just bought. He asked two shirt manufacturers about the fabric.

'Well, Mo' said one, 'if it's cotton it will flare up. If it's woollen, it will smoulder. Give us a spill of the fabric and we'll find out.'

Murgraff pulled his shirt from his trouser band and offered it. The shirt-maker flicked his lighter and put it to the shirt. A spurt of flame took hold, and spread. Murgraff yelled with pain and fright. Nearby diners jumped up and tore the shirt from him. Murgraff suffered a painful burn to his left forearm and a useful blow to his naivety. All his customers castigated the two shirt makers. When they had finished, the one who had set fire to the shirt said:

'Sorry Mo. Put your arm under cold running water. And, er, by the way . . . it definitely is cotton.'

After that, humorists would take out a cigarette and ask Mo for a light. He never thought this was funny. In truth, it was not. The shirtmakers were in bad odour with other customers for a long time for the cogent reason that had anything happened to Murgraff they would have lost a cherished lunchtime watering hole.

In the 1920s and 1930s the hours that later were spent in sitting and watching television were filled by indoor games and reading. Chess was the most widespread, followed by draughts, various games of dominoes, word games and board games played with dice, like ludo. But, everyone played cards. No one played cards with greater zest and passion than Dad and his circle. The game they all played was solo. Five nights a week Dad played solo in our house and away at his friends' homes. It was the high spot of gruelling anxious days of hard-working businessmen and enabled them to let off steam in the accusatory post-mortems that tended to follow each game played. The more acrimonious the rows, the more they enjoyed themselves. The unknown genius who invented the game of solo never knew the balming therapeutic effect he gave to thousands of the East End's immigrant Jews. Solo, as a subject for disputation, ran synagogue intrigues a very close second. As generals put out to grass regurgitated past battles so it was with those who played solo.

When it was Dad's night to host a card session the kitchen would be cleared to give central position to the fold-up green baized card table. Ceremoniously, Dad would place four chairs, dead centre on each side, and would then go to a drawer in the Welsh dresser that contained only packs of cards. He would select two packs and place them on the table and sit down to wait. That was the cue for Mum or Mary to place before him a plate, a sharp knife and a large pear. It was a fruit he adored above all others. He would polish it with a clean napkin, cut it into quarters, remove its core and pips and then demolish it slice by thin slice.

First in would be the rumbustious Mr Cohen, rubbing his hands in anticipation of an enjoyable disputatious evening. He would declare 'I feel lucky tonight, Yossele. Who else is coming?' My father would tell him, at which Mr Cohen would never let us down. He would snort disparagingly 'Ach. Those *kalikas* (idiots). They can't play so why did you ask them?'

Cohen laboured under the unshakeable belief that he was the best solo player in Hackney. When he lost, which was often, it was because his partners played like *lomen hagolem* (complete idiots) or that he had terrible cards. Or, because others cheated. Cohen must have had an overactive thyroid. He could never remain still, or composed. His reaction to any situation was instinctive. All this manifested itself in his passion for wireless. Even when he came into our house he would gravitate towards our wireless set, compulsively switch it on and turn the tuning dial. Once he caught Hitler making a speech live. That raucous demagoguic German raised such a storm, with Dad declaring angrily 'I won't hear that filthy voice in my house,' that Cohen reluctantly switched off the set. His subdued comment that we were listening to history being made cut no ice.

Kramer would arrive quietly, the inevitable small bowler perched foursquare on top of his head. He would raise it to the ladies and gravely wish everyone a polite good evening. Then, he would sit down at the cardtable, fold his arms and wait patiently. He was a dignified man, respected by everyone.

Nevertheless, his appearance gave Cohen a welcome distraction. He sat down next to Kramer and said sadly 'Ach, Kramer, my friend, it's amazing. You've been playing for so many years and you never improve. I hope you play better than you did last week when you accepted my proposition. If you had discarded your last useless diamond then you could have won an extra trick by trumping and we would have won instead of losing.'

Kramer had Cohen's measure. Cohen was fishing for an argument, lacking which, a difference of opinion to bite on. Kramer merely nodded acquiescence. Cohen was right. He, Kramer, had played badly. Frustrated, Cohen turned to Dad, steadfastly concentrating on the last of his pear. Cohen leaned back expansively and said 'Well, Yossel, where is he?' (it was always the more gentle 'Yossele' when Cohen was in tune with Dad and the harder 'Yossel' when otherwise). 'Why is he late? Are we going to sit here all night just waiting for him?'

'It's Chaim' said Dad. 'You know, he lays floors and carpets and maybe he has a late job.'

A dissatisfied Cohen was like hot lava in a volcanic crater, always rumbling, exploding dramatically and then cooling down again into a perceptible rumbling. When Chaim did arrive he apologised for being late. He did have to finish off a big job.

Cohen was having none of that. 'So?' He raised his arms and eyebrows. 'So? I, too, at times, work late. But I'm never late for a game to keep others waiting . . .'

'That's true, Isaac,' said Kramer gently, 'very true. Now, perhaps we can get on with the game?'

Solo requires four players. Each is dealt 13 cards from a shuffled pack hence, as in bridge, there are 13 tricks to be made. They play as individuals, not in partnership. The calling is as follows:

Pass: Poor hand, no call.

Proposition: If a player feels that with a partner he can make seven or more tricks, thus winning, he calls a prop.

Solo: if a player feels he can make five or more tricks in the trump suit playing against the other three.

Mizair: a very hard call to make. The player who calls it has to avoid making one single trick. If his opponents force him to make one, then he has lost.

Abundance: when a player has such a strong hand that, calling his own trumps, he feels he can make nine tricks.

It was the calling and not the actual playing that caused most dissension. Kramer's expression was always dead-pan. No one could tell whether he held good or bad cards. Dad could not prevent himself from looking dismayed or pleased at the hands dealt to him. Chaim sat back in his chair at a twisted angle as he sorted out his hand. He held the cards about two inches from his chest, as he peered down at them.

'Don't you trust us?' snorted Cohen.

'No.' Chaim was always a man of few words.

Cohen never bothered to conceal his feelings. When he slammed down on the table his folded cards and exclaimed 'Ach, God, what have I done to deserve this?' the others smiled. Once I saw him sit down in his chair and look like the cat which had swallowed the cream. He could not wait to call a triumphant solo. Then, Dad called a mizair, which superseded Cohen's solo. A cloud blotted out the sun. Cohen changed colour. Chaim swore later that steam came out of Cohen's ears. He glared at Dad and said with dangerous calm:

'So, Yossel. You have called a mizair. Why? Because I called a solo?'

Dad chuckled. 'I have a mizair, that's why I called it.'

Cohen, as calm as the eye of a hurricane, 'I do hope it's a strong one, Yossel. I hope you haven't called it because I called a solo. A cast iron solo . . .'

Kramer sighed. 'Is your solo that good, Isaac?'

Cohen: 'Good? Good?' His voice rose. 'I don't call *meshugenar* (mad) calls like Yossel.'

Kramer said gently 'It has been known to happen, Isaac.'

Chaim said 'For God's sake, Isaac, Yossel has called a mizair so let's play it.'

Having failed to bully Dad into retracting his call, Cohen played. Everyone prayed that Dad would avoid making a trick and win. But, undone by a freak card distribution, Dad lost. It was a moot point whether Cohen uttered a cry of anger or pain. Or both. He sat back and tugged at his beard and said:

'So, Yossel. You had a mizair. And a good one. Unbeatable . . .'

'It was a very good one,' protested Dad.

'Of course, Yossel.' The calm repetition of 'Yossel' by Cohen made everyone nervous. 'I saw how good it was. But, you lost . . .' Cohen's voice began to rise again. 'I had an eight trick solo. Not five, not six, not seven, but eight. And what do you do to me? You called a *meshuganer* mizair and ruin it. I'm your neighbour, Yossel, your friend, your guest . . .'

Cohen swung into full power. Mum, Mary, Freda and Rose vanished upstairs. Suddenly, Bessie appeared at the open kitchen window and screamed at her father to behave himself. Kramer pushed back his chair, splayed his long lean legs apart, folded his long thin arms, dropped his head on his chest and closed his eyes. His bowler, defying the laws of gravity, stayed on his head. Crouched behind a large armchair in the corner I kept quiet, enjoying every minute of it. Chaim went for a stroll in the garden. Dad picked up the *Evening News* and read it. Gradually Cohen subsided and then had the *chutzpah* to call Chaim in from the garden, telling him that he was holding up the play.

The prop and cop call caused most recrimination. Players with a weak hand sometimes succumbed to temptation and accepted a proposer whom they felt had a strong hand. The principle was sound. Better to stand a small chance of winning than the certainty of losing.

One evening Cohen accepted a prop by a Mr Rich, who owned two menswear shops. Cohen held a weak hand and should have passed. He and Rich were heavily defeated. Rich, one of the few immigrants to have mastered idiomatic English, took Cohen to task with Shakespearian explicitness. When he had finished Cohen, completely unruffled, stroked his luxurious beard and said with the sweetest of reasoning:

'What's the matter, Rich? Have you never accepted and gone down. There's no need to get so upset. After all, it's only a game . . .'

At which even the inscrutable Mr Kramer raised his face from his chest and cracked it into a slow wide smile.

Chapter Five

Every year early September ushered in the month of High Holydays and festivals. They dominated our lives. They commenced with *Rosh Hashana* (the New Year), followed by *Shabbat Shuva, Yom Kippur* (the Day of Atonement), *Succot* (the Feast of Tabernacles), *Shabbat Chol Hamoed, Hoshana Rabba, Shemini Atzeret* and finished on a high with the feasting, dancing, singing and bacchanalian shenanigans of *Simchat Torah* (the Celebration of the Law).

It was four weeks of gravitational ambiance pulling us back and holding us bound to the basic roots of Judaism, if only for that month. Decorum and piety reigned and there was a definite sense of occasion. I recall the steady trickles of grave, elderly men in their shiny top hats and sober suits walking to and from synagogues. There was always the frantic hunt for missing prayer books relevant to the Holyday we needed them for. I recall rushing home from synagogue and finding Mary in the scullery guarding the trays of food and mouth-watering freshly cooked foods. If we tried to scoop a wedge of chopped liver from the dish with our fingers or slice off a sliver of roast chicken or grab a dumpling Mary would foil us. She would swipe at errant hands with a wooden salad spoon and when it hit knuckles it was indeed painful. And she would admonish,

'While you boys have been resting on your backsides in shul your mother has been slaving over hot stoves. So . . . (whack, whack at Aubrey's furtive hand) you'll all just have to wait.'

Without realising it Mary was striking an early blow against male chauvinism. Sometimes Rose or Freda would come to her aid and push us out into the garden. Whereas we all rushed home, Dad tended to linger. He talked to this one, and to that one. He waited in the queues to shake hands with both the rabbi and the cantor. Then he would walk home slowly, often with Mr Cohen, commenting on the sermon, the choir, the windows that were never opened and any odd feature that had caught their attention. Once they could not get over the terrible affront to God when the musician son of Mr Reichbaum dared enter shul in a pearly-grey suit, jazzy tie and white dancing shoes. What an outrage! What next? Eventually, Dad would reach home. Mum would take him to task for keeping everyone waiting. Dad promised to be quicker home next time. He never was.

Even after Dad arrived back we still had to wait while he went upstairs and washed and changed into slippers and a comfortable jacket. Mick and I would play chess. Sam would fall into an armchair and doze off. Aubrey would hover by the food, watched by Mary. Mum and the girls would fret with impatience. When Dad appeared, oblivious to everyone's feelings, he said prayers before meals and, traditionally, tore slices of bread from the egg chollah for each of us, which we dipped into salt and ate. Ravenous Aubrey muttered 'Dad prays so much he doesn't give God a rest.'

In July 1940 I was posted as second radio officer to the SS Venetia, a tanker. I joined her at Stanley le Hope on the Thames. She was owned by a Clydeside shipping company. The Venetia was rusty, creaking and had been saved from the scrapyard by the war. She was old enough to have a forecastle with rows of hammocks for the sleeping quarters of the seamen and deckhands, and was overrun with cockroaches and rats.

My Scottish chief, Smithy, and I kept continuous watch, four hours on and four hours off, seven days a week. My other duties were daily attendance on 48 heavy duty wet batteries on monkey island, the roof of the chartroom which was open to the elements. In high seas and heavy winds the wet planking and the Venetia's *violent movements had me slithering and falling as I topped up cells with distilled water, checked lashings, scraped oxidisation from insulators, and greased terminals. I was perpetually soaked, bruised and hungry. But never tired.*

At 0400 hours every morning when Smithy relieved me I staggered down to my wardrobe-sized cabin and fell onto my bunk in trousers and sweater. I put the thick heavy wooden door onto a heavy latch, which kept it ajar. If we were torpedoed or hit a mine and the door jammed I would never get out. At 0730 the assistant steward roused me for breakfast before I went back on watch at 0800 hours. For the first five days I was too sick to consider food. Then, as we rounded Pentland Firth, I woke up ravenous, all sickness gone. I hurried into the amidships saloon and into the inescapable grip of upbringing. Before me was placed one sunny side up egg and two frizzled pieces of bacon. Oh, how I groaned. I ate the egg. Jimmy Wallace, my shipmate, grinned and took my bacon as he advised me to fill up on bread.

The bread, for me, was inedible. It was sour-white and sprinkled with specks which upon close examination proved to be bits of careless cockroaches which had been caught up in the dough. Others smothered the thick slices in butter and jam and downed them. I could not. The tea came in large white enamelled mugs. It was nectar.

Jimmy, my age, took me under his protective wing when I joined the ship. He told me he was very glad I had joined the ship as morning after morning he ate my bacon. When pork chops were served, he had those as well. A week out from Oban in a transatlantic convoy I said that if he wanted my bacon I wanted his egg. Alas, Jimmy could not forego his egg. I was so hungry, even though by then I was forcing slabs of that bread down my throat, cockroach pieces and all. One morning I closed my eyes and silently begged Dad's forgiveness and nibbled a crumb of bacon. It was too alien to my taste. Jimmy grinned as he took my bacon and said 'Tut tut, Sparky. Bacon is not for you.'

The taste lingered in my mouth for a long time. I felt so guilty. It was ridiculous and I knew it, but I was letting everyone down, God, my religion, myself and, above all, Dad. I was so fit and working so hard and so ravenous all the time. Hunger began to defeat guilt. I started to get more and more of the bacon down, concealing its taste inside thick slices of bread. I wondered whether cockroaches were permissibly kosher. Poor Jimmy. He took his loss of a daily bonus portion of bacon in good spirit.

When we berthed at Saint Nicholas in Aruba, in the Dutch West Indies, I went ashore with Jimmy and we spent all our drawn money on chocolates, mainly Hershey bars, and fruit. When we left Aruba laden with some 9,000 tons of high octane fuel destined for the petrol tanks of Spitfires and Hurricanes I was downing all my bacon, albeit without too great an enthusiasm. I could never stomach pork, nor ham. Yet, an important restraint had been severed for all time.

Leaving Bermuda after no shore leave, we weighed anchor and joined a homeward-bound convoy. Crossing east of longitude 30° west we entered U-boat alley, the recognised danger zone. Just before dawn one morning we were attacked by a U-boat pack. I was awakened by explosions, ships' sirens blowing the emergency short blasts, shouts and running feet. I donned tunic, jacket, greatcoat, cap and the neck-breaker lifejacket. It comprised two cubes of cork, one in front and one behind. Unless you held them down when you jumped into water they would rise under your jaw and break your neck. Parachute flares fired by the U-boats were descending slowly, silhouetting merchantmen into easy targets. Here and there I saw burning ships. Jimmy joined me on the welldeck. We stared at the Norwegian tanker that had been on our starboard bow and was now falling behind us. She was an inferno, covered by a deep red glow from which a wide oily swathe of black smoke reached to the low clouds. Its fuel storage tanks had been holed. Oil must have been gushing out. Small fires around the sinking ship spread and joined. I saw men jumping from the tanker into the burning waters. Another rumbling explosion ahead and I saw a British ship savaged by a tall sheet of flame, followed by smoke. She keeled over as if pushed. U-boat ahead. The Venetia *swung hard to port. My eyes swung back to the burning Norwegian tanker and realising that we carried a similar inflammable cargo I found myself muttering in Hebrew that final prayer of Jews over the centuries, who have faced death:*

'Hear O Israel. The Lord our God, the Lord is One.'

'Did you say something?' muttered Jimmy.

'No.'

'Liar.' He nudged me. 'Well, Sparky, what do you prefer? Drowning or burning?'

I prayed under my breath. When convoys were attacked and devastated, they scattered. It was their only defence. We headed due north at a painful maximum speed of nine knots. Before we got clean away we heard and saw two more distant torpedo strikes. Much later that day, completely alone, we saw in the distance a surfaced U-boat shelling a merchantman. We turned away sharply to starboard. A Sunderland flying boat circled low overhead and aldis-lamped us to follow a certain course. We did and later that night joined seven other merchant ships being escorted by one destroyer. In due course we reached the Clyde and anchored off Blairmore in Loch Long.

To our dismay we received orders to discharge cargo into the tanks at Shellhaven, back in the Thames, so one chilly daybreak we joined a convoy of ships bound for discharge of their cargoes into east coast British ports. I had become friends with a Spanish able-seaman. He had been a left-wing journalist and had fought against Franco and thus could never return home. Twice a week when I came off watch at 0400 hours I would sneak along to the forecastle where we would play chess and he would teach me Spanish. To reach the forecastle from the radio cabin amidships I had to make my way along the fly-bridge. This was a wooden yard-wide platform running ten feet above the well-deck. A lifeline, threaded through the eyes of metal stanchions, ran its length. Use of the fly-bridge at all time required that at least one hand held onto the lifeline. With the weight of the cargo the Venetia's welldeck was perpetually under water in comparatively calm seas.

One morning we were rounding Cape Wrath in filthy weather when I left the radio cabin to go to the forecastle. Rushing waves were slopping their tops across the fly-bridge. I thought of not going, then I kept my tryst with the Spaniard. At about 0500 hours I left the forecastle. The welldeck was completely under water, driven by a fierce wind. Momentarily careless, I took my hand off the lifeline just as a hostile swell angled the **Venetia**. *I slipped and slithered off the fly-bridge. I screamed. In a panic, I flung out both arms. My right hand cracked against the bottom of a stanchion and I clung to it. Water rushed over me, dragging me seaward. I hauled myself back onto the fly-bridge and lay there, face pressed against the planks. The ship was blacked out. A low cloud base obscured the moon and the stars. No one could have seen me.*

The next day the knuckle and lower joint of my right hand little finger swelled up, then my wrist and arm. The Geordie captain gave me hell for my stupidity. I kept watch, aided by my chief, and maintained the batteries with the help of Jimmy. At Shellhaven I hurried ashore to see a doctor. He sent me to a hospital where the bones were manipulated, splinted and put in plaster. I was replaced. Jimmy helped me ashore with my baggage and we had a last meal together in a dreary cafe. We both ordered specials which comprised eggs, bacon, tomatoes, sausages and chips. Jimmy chided me,

'You? Bacon and pork sausage?'

I lifted them onto his plate and smiled 'You greedy sod. I hope my replacement has hollow arms and legs. We'll keep in touch. You've been a great friend.'

'You, too' said Jimmy sadly.

A long handshake. Promises to write and keep in touch and then I watched Jimmy trudge back to the ship. Much later I was home on survivor's leave. It had been six months since I had bade Jimmy goodbye at Shellhaven. Apart from an early postcard from Curaçao there was no mail from Jimmy. I phoned Gow Harrison and Co. in Glasgow and spoke to the office manager. He was wary at first. I gave him my name, rank, paybook number and details about various **Venetia** crew members and he opened up.

'After you left her' he said, 'and no one else did, she went back to the West Indies. On the way home she was torpedoed. There were no

survivors. You'll never hear from Jimmy Wallace again. I'm sorry.'
    'God' I sighed. 'Lucky I fell off the fly-bridge.'
    'Aye' said the Scot. 'There must be something in Jews' luck after all.'

Back to the 1930s and the month of High Holydays. For Dad and his male contemporaries it was a roller-coasting high of excitement and intense personal fulfilment. For Mum, Mary and my two sisters it was hard work, a never ending round of shopping, preparing food, cooking, laying the dining room tables for meals and washing up. Duster whisked, furniture was waxed and linoleum was mopped and polished. Mary scrubbed the stone steps outside the front door until they gleamed white. She red-leaded the hearth tiles and blacked the grates. She rebelled once, when she opened that massive chest in the lower passage and slammed it shut with the lament 'What a mess. I can't do anything with it.'

That chest. It was of dark-stained oak, six feet long, two feet wide and two feet deep. Everyone put things into it and never took them out again. It was a jumble of discarded clothing, cricket boots, plimsolls, Mick's discarded ukelele, hats, old bags, unwashed football shirts and shorts, a wizened coconut, dozens of shrivelled old conkers and recollections of our childhoods such as maimed moth-eaten teddy bears, toys and remains of a meccano set. But that chest was an invaluable accomplice to my brothers and I. On Saturdays, when we had to get away to play football and cricket for our schools, we packed the bags and hid them in the chest, to retrieve after return from synagogue and dinner and scoot from the house while Mum distracted Dad's attention elsewhere. Returning later that day we would put the bags back into the chest. During muddy weather the mud-encrusted shirts and shorts would stand up by themselves. Mary would take mine and wash them, to the chagrin of Mick and Aubrey. She would tell them they were big and ugly enough to wash their own. Sometimes Rose and Freda would do it for them, but never Mary.

The two September festivals I enjoyed most were *Succot* and *Simchat Torah*. A *succah* was a shed built in back gardens to a specific design. The roof opened to the skies. It comprised two side pieces which, when opened, went right back until they were vertical, and when closed rested against a central longitudinal crossbeam. Every Jewish family with a back garden had one. Just below roof level was a wooden lattice-work. The day before the festival commenced Rose, Freda and Mary overlaid the latticework with leaves and small branches and tied all manner of fruits to dangle from it. In sunny weather it was almost romantic to eat beneath that canopy of fruit and leaves. Our *succah* was at the end of the back garden. We ate the midday and evening meals there. While Mum served up in the scullery Mary, Rose and Freda trotted up the garden path with the food and back with the empties. Not even the last wasps of summer buzzing lethargically about our heads could spoil the picnic atmosphere. It never seemed to rain during *Succot* week. Mum never ate with the family in the *succah*, but with Mary at a small table in the kitchen.

Mary appreciated this. When Mum took her afternoon rest in the armchair in the kitchen she would do so with her sewing box and a pile of garments needing repairs on chairs beside her. With her spectacles halfway down her nose she darned, repaired holes, turned collars, sewed on buttons, lengthened and shortened and took in and let out. The pile rose and diminished but I never saw it completely cleared. She always fell asleep while working. Mary knew this. She watched Mum like a hawk and when Mum dozed off she gently removed whatever needle and cotton she held and would then keep everybody out of the kitchen. We all had to tip-toe about.

A treasured memory of *Succot* was to see the men in their

shiny top hats and cutaway black suits going to synagogue clutching their *lulavs* (spears of long sharp leaves bound tightly together) and their *etrogs* (large inedible citrons), which they required for various responses throughout the service. When they raised the *lulavs* on high it was a medieval army saluting God. How Dad lapped up the awesome protectiveness of the Almighty. The outside world of worry, disappointments and daily drudgery was shut out until he walked home and saw the anti-semitic slogans daubed on walls by blackshirts and the gloom-laden newspaper placards.

Oh, the amount of human energy that revolved around food – the shopping, preparing, eating, washing up after it and talking about it. We ate more fish than meat. It was cheaper. Our fishmonger kept fish alive in large aerated tanks. Sometimes, when Mum tipped them out onto the guttering and chopping board, they wriggled and even leaped into the air. Rose and Freda would pull faces and vanish. Mary would exclaim 'Ugh. Poor things. I don't think I can eat them after this.'

Once a week Mum would buy quantities of herrings for pickling. After gutting and cleaning them she laid them in a large deep metal tray which she placed outside under the garden water tap. She liked to leave the tap running over the herrings for about 20 minutes. I was deputed to stand guard over them. Cats were the enemy, attracted by the smell, alerted I am sure by a feline bush telegraph, and they soon appeared. My presence frustrated them. I could sense their hostility as I waved a cricket stump around at the circle of yellow-eyed predators. I have never known such boy-hating feral cats. I often wondered what I would do if they launched a concerted attack to get at the fish. I think I would have deserted my post very speedily.

Every Tuesday Mum had her day off. It was sacrosanct and not even the High Holydays, unless it was *Yom Kippur*, could interfere with it. A short rest after the midday meal, then she would don her best clothes and sally forth to meet her two friends, Mincha and Toapcha. They usually met where Amhurst Road ran into Stoke Newington High Street. They would go to a pre-selected film and sink luxuriously into seats where no one could make demands of them. They nibbled chocolates and chewed toffees. After the film they would make their way to the Lyons tea shop by Dalston Junction and have a high tea with buttered scones and jam, pastries and even a hot sweet like a jam roll with custard. When Mum eventually came home she looked rested and happy. Alas, the next day she would look her usual tired self again.

At last it came round. *Simchat Torah*. Let merriment be unconfined, and it was. Released from the austerity that characterised the more sober High Holydays, everyone acted a little crazily and none more so than hitherto constrained boys. Now, for one day, we could get away with murder and this we did. Nowhere were high jinks higher than in the intimate Dalston Talmud Torah in Amhurst Road, before Dad upped stakes and joined the more decorous Stoke Newington synagogue.

Inside the Talmud Torah tables were set up with a feast of fried fish balls, gefilte fish, small viennas, sandwiches, biscuits, fruit and strudels and bottles of that red sweetish Carmel wine. As the food and drink went down the congregants became less inhibited. They sang lively liturgical songs with accompanying foot-stamping, hand-clapping and alcoholic goodwill to all fellow Jews. Faces flushed and dripped with perspiration. Prayer shawls were used to wipe brows and faces. Expensive top hats tilted precariously and some fell off. Tragedy struck when they were trodden upon, and this always happened to somebody.

There were a dozen and one mischiefs boys could get up to. Our inventiveness knew no bounds. Threads were strung across doorways and more top hats were swept to the ground. Food was sabotaged in various ways; mustard was inserted and small squares of cardboard were concealed between folded smoked salmon. Once, everyone was electrified by an anguished shout from a Mr Romania, who owned a news-agent and tobacconist shop in Sandringham Road. He had bitten into an apple and broken a tooth. A boy had carefully sliced a small wedge from the apple, cut away a little of the inside flesh and inserted a small stone into the hole. Then, he had pressed the cut piece back so well that only a close inspection would have revealed the join. Of course, Mr Romania had just grabbed the apple and bit hard into it.

Drawing pins on chairs and crawling under them to tie shoe laces together were commonplace. A most rewarding prank was the tying together of tassels belonging to two different prayer shawls. When the victims moved apart the shawl would be jerked from one shoulder. The victim would jerk it back and, in doing so, pull the *tallit* from his neighbour's shoulder. He, in turn, would tug it back, and so on. One genius lost himself in the cloakroom and stitched up the buttonholes in several coats. When the congregants, lost in a haze of food and wine and bonhomie, went to collect their coats some could not fathom out why their buttons did not go through the holes. It was hilarious for those not affected. When the victims realised the cause of their misfortunes boys became bad news and the wise boys made themselves scarce.

When the month of festivals had run its course we all felt we had run a marathon. Back at school, our gentile friends observed enviously 'Cor. You've been away a lot this month.'

'It's our religion.'

'You Jews have all the luck.'

Jews' luck. The luck of the Irish. Everyone except the Jews and Irish think they possess it.

Early in the spring of 1938 Aubrey and Mick, along with other members of London Maccabi's first cricket XI, resigned after a dispute and set up their own team. They called it The Yorkers. The players wore chocolate-coloured blazers with

63

caps to match. It was the first all-Jewish team to play outside the Jewish Sunday leagues. It played on Sundays and had a brief life of two seasons. The Yorkers had no home ground so every fixture was played away and they played first class club teams like Gerrards Cross, Ealing Dean, Potters Bar, Midhurst, Edmonton and the Indian Gymkhana at Osterley.

They attracted a collection of talented players, some of whom with dedication, could have made county standard. It was a team of brothers. There were the Allens, Len and Bernie, who later ran their own estate agency and property management business. Len was an extremely fast bowler who could swing the ball two ways. He was always given the ball to demolish tail-enders. Bernie, a tall genial giant played wicket keeper. He was also a middle order batsman. He had a very long reach and intense concentration and when told to stay there, usually managed to do so. There were the two South African brothers, Herbert and Alfred Green, both high scoring batsmen. Alf opened the batting with Aubrey and they put up quite a few century plus opening stands. There were the Clarfelts, Jack and Sid, our neighbours in Hackney. Jack was a steady batsman and an agile cover point, able to pick up the ball, throw it on the run and hit the stumps for a run out. Sid was a steady batsman and safe fielder. There was Aubrey and Mick and, when I played a few games for The Yorkers, three Beckmans in the team. Mick was one of two spin bowlers. He bowled left arm over. He could bowl a googly and an unexpectedly fast leg break which would cut in behind the batsman's legs and hit the wicket. Mick was a ferocious competitor, his appealing outrageously intimidating. If he failed to win an appeal he would throw his arms into the air with the most histrionic incredulity. If a fielder dropped a catch off his bowling he would stand, hands on hips, glaring at him. 'If looks could kill,' observed Herbert Green, 'Mick would wipe out the whole team several times over.'

There was Nat Fenton, tall and quiet, who batted at number

three. During the war he joined the parachute regiment and it was said that he was killed in Normandy. Rufus Quas-Cohen, a Yorkshireman, had played wicket keeper for the army. There was Leslie Luck, just a little older than myself. He was a very hard hitting batsman and a very fast outfielder. He joined the RAF, won his wings and became a fighter pilot in a Hurricane squadron. He was shot down and killed in the Battle of Britain. London Maccabi instituted a Leslie Luck football trophy which Jewish clubs in the Sunday League played for.

There was the saxophonist who played in a big band and turned out when engagements permitted. He was a naggingly accurate bowler with the ability to maintain perfect length and line. Marcel Morris, Marzy as he was affectionately known, was a competent all rounder. He was a constant practical joker who manufactured caps and hats. During the war, which he survived, he flew as a navigator with bomber command. There were others whose names I have forgotten. It was a happy team.

Because fixtures were made by correspondence and the letterhead was headed Yorkers Cricket Club, our opponents usually had no idea that we were a Jewish club until we arrived. Some of the clubs did not ban Jews from joining but, somehow, when applicants had to pass through the sieve of the select committees, Jews did not pass. When we arrived there were some clubs where we evoked discomfort, even embarrassment. But both teams were there, so we always played. A few of the clubs were salted with county players and could not conceal their anticipation of a quick win.

This instilled in us a terrible will to win. We felt that we could save many runs per match by perfecting our fielding. Our efforts showed in the full length slides to stop boundaries and the ball being thrown low and hard to just above the stumps for Bernie to whip off the bails. We won many games and, in fairness, many of the clubs we played invited us back for a following season's fixture.

On the field we made it *de rigeur* for the team to comport itself in a sporting and gentlemanly manner. The one blot on this escutcheon was the competitive Mick. His appetite for taking wickets was so voracious. Once, I heard Rufus Quas-Cohen admonish him despairingly,

'Mick. You're a bloody good spin bowler but you're not a gentleman. Now, if an umpire turns down your appeal, swear at him, if you must but not so that he bloody well hears you.'

Mary made the sandwiches for Aubrey and Mick to take with them when they played. When I clamoured to be taken with and they told me to get lost Mary would blackmail them: 'Take him with you. Or, no sandwiches.' She would even walk out to Mick's car to see that they did take me. They accepted my presence with good-humoured resignation. Before the game they had me bowling to them. Sometimes, joy of joys, they gave me a bat and bowled to me. They felt I could play a bit and paid me the compliment of bowling their fastest, even though I wore no pads, box or gloves. It sharpened my reflexes no end.

Chapter Six

In the early 1930s I won a place in Hackney Downs Secondary school, more popularly known as The Grocers. It had a merited scholastic reputation and was the local school all parents wanted their sons to get into. It was a family red letter day when I donned the school uniform; a navy blazer with badge and the navy cap with two parallel encircling yellow bands that met the badge in the front of the cap. The school badge, embroidered in yellow thread, had a camel carrying a load of cloves. Grey knee high stockings and black shoes completed the ensemble.

The founders of the company which founded the school were known as pepperers because they traded in spices and peppers from the east. They were mainly wholesalers and it was an easy linguistic slide for the company to be known as The Grocers. In 1345 King Edward III granted a Charter of Incorporation to The Grocers Company and its foundation took place. Among the first 20 names registered as belonging to the company was John William Grantham who, in 1327, became Lord Mayor of London.

In 1873 the Court of Assistants of the Worshipful Company of Grocers agreed to spend £30,000 on a school in north London. They selected a site in Hackney Downs and in 1876 the building was completed. There were 120 applicants for the job of headmaster. Chosen was Herbert Courthope Bowen, a mathematical prizeman of Corpus Christi College, Cambridge, who was twice made university prizeman in English. He was the first in the line of top rate headmasters. In 1876 the school opened with 210 boys, each paying an entrance fee of £1 per term plus an annual tuition fee of £6. 5s. From that solid start the school soon developed an enviable reputation for learning and sporting achievement.

The enclosure of part of Hackney Downs for the two playgrounds was resented by locals. One riotous day they tore down the fences which the school had erected on one of the lammas lands of Hackney. From 16 April to 11 August each year freehold tenants of the manor had exclusive rights to graze their cattle on the lush knee-high lammas grass. Each year, a body called Marsh Drivers were elected at the courts of the manor to manage the lammas grazing lands. They charged a small fee for every head of cattle turned out to graze by the local freeholders, each of whom marked out his site with posts. Thus, the enclosure of land by the school hit pockets and aroused local enmity. Yet, the school became a respected local amenity as Hackney's population burgeoned.

When I joined The Grocers it had upwards of 700 pupils. They were divided into six houses; Greens, Hammonds, Pickfords, Brittens, Richards and Lucas. Each house was managed by a housemaster, and competed fiercely to emerge as top dog in every sphere of activity from chess to gymnastics to football and cricket. Pride in one's house was as natural as breathing and partisanship was uninhibited. That intense rivalry spurred many of us on to that little bit better. The school imbued into us the spirit that while losing was no disgrace, lacking the will and effort to try to win certainly was.

Sam had left the school long before I joined it. Aubrey was still there, in the Upper Fifth. He was in the school first XIs at both football and cricket and was regarded as a star in both. When he graciously let me walk home with him, I was very proud, even though when he was with another boy he insisted that I did not speak.

Chapter Six

Very quickly I felt the subtle change of emphasis. Sigdon Road elementary was the educational equivalent of the square bashing camp where basics were hammered into our brains. The Grocers was the springboard into future careers. New boys were immediately made aware of the two important hurdles to leap; Matriculation and then Higher Schols, with the outside chance of winning a state scholarship to Oxford or Cambridge. Dad suddenly became far more interested in my school reports. Homework was heavy and there was no going out to play until it was finished.

My contemporaries and I began to wonder for the first time about future careers. The professions loomed large with medicine, law and accountancy being the favourites. The arts, music, acting and even film-making came into the frame. Yet, a persistent distraction was the rise of fascism in Europe. Copycat anti-semitism in Hackney became more discernible. A threat, however distant, can be pushed temporarily aside but never ignored.

About this time I became more aware of the extent of my own family. I never imagined that I had so many cousins. Most exciting was the discovery that Mum had a brother in Rotterdam, married, with two sons and a daughter. But the special affinity I had was with Mum's youngest sister, Aunt Golda. Perhaps it was a case of youngest bonding to youngest.

Golda had married a man whose surname was Rose. I never met him, nor knew what he did. They had one son, Harry. Mr Rose died suddenly at a young age. Golda married again to a quiet personable man to whom we all took. His name was Jack Rosengarten. He was noted for his hobby. In a workshop added to his house he made the most exquisite miniature antique furniture, perfect to scale and detail. A chest of drawers was filled with illustrations, photographs and neat sketches which he had made in museums and stately homes. One whole wall was covered by miniature tools, many of which he had devised himself. The neat stacks of

69

veneers and woods, the bubbling pots of glues and resins turned my mind towards the evident satisfactions of creativity with one's hands. Uncle Jack worked with a dexterity and concentration that I envied. When I remarked on it he smiled, 'To concentrate as I do, you have to really love what you are doing. Which I do.' Tragically, he died young from a massive heart attack. Aunt Golda never married again.

She lived for her son, Harry. Older than me by a few years, he was no great achiever. He went from job to job; chauffeur, warehouseman, salesman in a men's outfitters and so on. As long as he earned enough to enable him to watch the Arsenal, play snooker and go dancing at the Hammersmith Palais or Lyceum, he was content.

Came the war Harry went into the army. He went out to India and then onto Burma where as an infantry sergeant he saw action at the battles of Imphal and Kohima. His air letters home always assured his mother that he was having a safe time in India. She never quite believed what they said. He volunteered to fight for the Chindit Force, led by General Wingate, which operated offensively behind the Japanese lines. Later, he told me how frightened he had been on many occasions.

'The worst' he said,

> *was at night. The jungle was so humid I'd be soaked in sweat and with the canopy of trees overhead it was so bloody pitch black I couldn't see my hand in front of my face. On sentry duty I'd crouch with my bayonet fixed and my back against a tree. There would be all sorts of noises and insects kept landing on my face and hands. My eyes played tricks and my mind played tricks. The Japs could have been within yards of me and I'd never have known. Sometimes, I was out of my mind with fear. I often wanted to open fire at what I imagined were movements . . . I didn't want to make a fool of myself and I didn't want to give away our position. The Japs could have been anywhere . . . any-*

way, it's all behind. I've got the Arsenal, snooker, the occasional pint and birds galore. What more could a man fight for or want?

Harry never climbed mountains, or wanted to. He knew his limitations and stayed within them. He never did harm to anyone. He smiled easily and his years in the army enabled him to fulfil his one and only ambition, to return to the life he had left behind when he joined it.

Six years after the war I was in partnership with a man 20 years my senior. We manufactured men's clothing and were establishing a profitable business. Aunt Golda phoned me. She sounded troubled. Harry had married a divorcee with two children. They lived in Southend. Now, Harry had to earn money to keep four. He wanted to open a menswear shop just off the High Street. Could I help him?

For Aunt Golda, anything. I drove to Southend. Harry was no longer the handsome, lean bronzed warrior in bush hat back from Burma. He was thinner and strained by the need to earn more money. I agreed to support his shop venture with stocks. Back in London, my partner agreed that we should help him. I filled my car with stock and drove back to Southend. This time Harry was excited and optimistic. He was sure he would make a go of it. For two years he struggled and always lagged behind on payment. We never pressed him. His cheques always went through. He was trying. Then, I learned from his mother that he was having domestic troubles. His wife left him for another man. His business went bankrupt and we lost just over £1,000. Harry phoned. He was upset. He would make it up, he swore it. I gave my partner a personal cheque to cover his share of the loss. He tore up the cheque.

Aunt Golda phoned me again. She sounded despairing. Could I help Harry? We supplied a chain of menswear shops, Smart and Weston. I managed to get Harry a job as a leading salesman in their large Kingsland Road shop. Harry's basically sunny personality worked with customers and I was told he was doing well. Then, within a week he moved into a flat with a childless woman in Clapton and left his job. Somehow, he became an underbuyer in the Hounds-

ditch Warehouse Company. He had a bad car accident and suffered amputation below the knee of his right leg. He dropped out of sight. He never contacted me again. For a while he lived with his mother. She never spoke about him. Then I heard that he had died. What of, and why, I never knew. After that Aunt Golda became very reclusive. She never went out and made it plain that she did not want to see any of the family. Harry was not the wisest or luckiest person in the world.

Aunt Tamara married a hard-working grocer named Lewis. They both were quiet and hospitable people. They had two sons, David and Arnold, who both went into the army and survived the war.

Mum's third sister, Rose, married a Mr Gordon, a wealthy manufacturer of men's clothing. They had two daughters, Pearl and Sadie, and lived in a large multi-roomed corner house in The Vale, Golders Green.

Pearl was an attractive brunette, elegant, svelte and fastidious to the nth degree in all that she wore, ate and did. She gave her many suitors a hard time. Eventually, she married and, not too many years later, divorced. She moved away from London and out of contact with the rest of the family. Her young sister Sadie was a gauche large lump of a girl. She was plain, bespectacled and shy. But she was highly intelligent and very determined and she gave the family two intriguing talking points. She started and successfully built up her own business, a startling and tremendous achievement for a girl in those days, and she married what Dad termed a mystery. His name was Harold. He was, looking back, a playboy. He never seemed to work hard and he was never short of money. He confounded the prevailing Jewish attitudes to work by actually playing golf on weekdays. He drove expensive sports cars, which he had the ability to maintain himself. His favourite dress was a navy blazer, grey worsted slacks and a white silk scarf tucked round his neck. He made frequent trips abroad. He and Sadie were very happy together but they were tight-lipped and never divulged any information about themselves to the curious, or nosey. They had one daughter, a tall willowy girl, almost a facsimile of Pearl.

Golda. Tamara. Rose. Mum's fourth sister was Hannah, a severely conscientious and taciturn woman, completely over-shadowed by a dominant husband. He owned a shop in Walthamstow. As was par for the course in those days they lived above the shop. They sired a son who turned out to be one of the family's blackest sheep or one of its greatest characters. Opinion on this was largely governed by age group.

Jack Frauenglass was born unlucky. God had endowed him with so many bonuses that the total sum added up to a handicap. He was the most incredibly sexy, powerful, good-looking man. Put him alongside his careworn parents and you would shake your head and say that he could not possibly be their son. Women called him a film star. In the 1930s when only God and Hollywood created stars that was the highest of accolades. He was very strong with muscular shoulders tapering down to a narrow waist. He had a luxuriant mane of wavy black hair, a straight-nosed chin-jutting profile, liquid black eyes and, as if God had not dished out enough goodies to one person, dimples in both cheeks.

He spoke softly in a cultured resonant voice. Oozing the self-confidence of an Adonis aware of his effect on others he was utterly unflappable. His achilles heel was the distress that he knew he caused to his orthodox principled parents. He strove to palliate this with a stream of flowers and presents, which he sent them from wherever he happened to be. He was a five star success with girls and never had to learn about sex in school. He adored Mum and would pop into Amhurst Road and with a rapturous 'And how's my favourite Auntie?' would embrace her and plant a smacking kiss on her cheek. Mary would stare at him with an expression that said it all.

73

Jack was physically very strong and he kept himself that way by working out in gymnasiums where he became friendly with many of the boxing and wrestling fraternities. For some years he was a bosom friend of Eric Boon, a British welterweight champion at the time. No one quite knew what he did for a living, although it was known that he took work as a film extra and even played minor parts. He did let slip to my brother Sam that he performed stunts, some of which were classified as dangerous, for which he was well paid.

His father was always grim about his son's wasted life. Jack found it too easy to wallow in the hedonism that was his for the taking and lacked the will to knuckle down to trying to qualify for a profession. In effect, he shirked hard work of the drudging kind. What really upset Jack's father was when he felt the name Frauenglass did not suit his image and changed it to Jack Beckman. His father never reconciled himself to this act of treachery. Over the 1930s and 1940s Jack married three, or four, actresses. Not one of them was Jewish. He had no children. His ageing father would shake his head and say 'Ach. He's wasted his whole life. And for what?'

Jack never went into the forces during the war. It was said that he failed his medical for a malfunctioning middle ear. This went down ill with his male relatives who, without exception, served in the forces. For Jews it was an inescapable duty to fight the Nazis. However, during the war Jack did a bit of this and a bit of that, and he made money. In 1944 he was running a night club off Leicester Square. The combination of allied officers, especially Americans, women and whisky galore, was better than printing money. Nat took me there once when I came home. Jack greeted me very warmly and told the staff that everything we had was on the house. It was a packed, noisy and fractious place. Nat told me of the happening that had virtually become a legend.

One evening a group of drunken American officers began throwing verbal white feathers at any man in civilian clothes. Some of their targets were servicemen who had donned civvies to enjoy their leave. They resented the barbs being thrown their way. To nip trouble in the bud Jack asked the Americans to behave themselves. Jack was in a tuxedo and this, combined with his looks and attraction for the women, brought out the redneck in one of the Americans. He said perceptively 'Why aren't you in uniform you fucking kike?' That did it.

Jack was always the most active of action men. He said to the bouncer by the door 'Please, George, would you hold the door open?', then he grabbed the offending American and threw him out onto the pavement. He grabbed a second, and did likewise. The others got to their feet to set about Jack. He knocked them down one by one and one after the other he threw their befuddled bodies out into the street before a circle of appreciative counting onlookers. The night Jack Beckman ejected seven officers from the club single-handed was a remembered event.

When the war ended every demobilised serviceman wanted a car. This resulted in boom time for the second hand car market, and Warren Street, off Tottenham Court Road, became the place to buy one. Along its entire length on both sides kerbside dealers offered their bargains. Jack was one of the first in. He operated from there for several years. He did well and then slipped out of the family frame. Years later, I met him at a family wedding. The hair had greyed and thinned. The cheeks were sunken in and he stooped a little but the old bravura was there, so was the charm and the dimples. He said that he was living in a bedsit in St Johns Wood and that we must meet again. We never did. Jack was never a bore. He was telling me about the thriving wartime black market, then he said unexpectedly, 'When you were on a petrol tanker didn't you ever feel angry about bastards like me making money out of petrol coupons?' I answered honestly that we never even knew about it, that we were getting paid for doing a job and that we were more concerned about the lousy ship food and having a rave up when we got to port.

The British Merchant Navy did have a torrid time. It lost 2,524 ships and suffered 45,329 casualties, of whom 30,248 were killed, in

75

World War II. The two years which I spent criss-crossing the Atlantic, covering the period which the U-boats called their Happy Time, our convoys were attacked going and coming. Every attack cost ships and lives. I recall being caught up in fights that broke out in dockside pubs when uniformed servicemen, drunk, would taunt merchant navymen for not being in the armed forces. The seamen, who had survived U-boat attacks, bombs, mines and German raiders on the loose, not to speak of dangerously overladen ships, reacted predictably. More than a few dockside pubs were wrecked by the ensuing fights. Which is why the government issued lapel aluminium MN badges for seamen to wear ashore. When seamen were asked what the MN under the crown meant they replied it was for monkey nuts. It became known as the monkey nut badge.

The greatest scandal to hit the family the 1930s was the Henry Beckman affair. Dad's nephew Henry qualified as a chartered accountant. From all accounts he was brilliant, hard-working and ambitious. Very. He was making a name for himself in the City. He acquired important clients, became their friends, and through their recommendations picked up more important clients. He was always attending dinners and banquets. He fell in love with a ravishingly beautiful East End girl and, everyone agreed on this, she was so stunning that when she entered a room or hall she would turn all heads. They married and had two sons. At first, all went well. But Kitty despite her looks was a simple East End girl with *Hausfrau* ambitions. She lacked the desire to raise her sights and to accompany and match her high-flying husband. She could not, or would not, improve. Henry found it increasingly embarrassing to take her to black tie functions where he made contacts useful to his progress. They quarrelled. Soon, he was going to functions on his own. Kitty did not like the idea of playing second fiddle to her husband's career, No one knew, of course what transpired in their home but the marriage did become stormy.

Chapter Six

One morning, Henry left home for his office. He never reached it. Nor did he return home. Imaginations ran riot until a week after he disappeared my brother Sam received a letter from him. It was post-marked Paris. It read 'When you receive this letter you will know that I am never returning home. I enclose my season ticket for the Spurs as you enjoy football as much as I do.'

What a storm of conjecture that letter unleashed. Had he planned the move or was it a sudden brainstorm that made him do it? He was by then a very wealthy man. He was in no financial difficulty. He was politically-minded and it was felt that he would have achieved honours as well as wealth. He never returned to England. He never wrote another letter or card to any member of the family. Rumours trickled in that he had been seen in America, South Africa, the Argentine, even in Palestine. The one thing that damned him in all eyes was that he had deserted a wife with two small children. Kitty, at first, was helped by the family. But she turned very bitter and cut herself off from all social contact with them. Long after the war I heard that her two sons had both qualified as chartered accountants. The family wounds never healed even though everyone apart from Henry were innocent parties.

Late in 1941 I was second radio officer on the SS *Trojan Star. We went down to Buenos Aires to bring back foodstuffs and general cargo. My first task ashore was to find a telephone. In a directory I came across two Beckmans. Thanks to the tuition of the Spanish able-seaman on the* Venetia *I could just about make myself understood. Neither had any knowledge of any Henry Beckman.*

Some three years later, after recovering from paratyphoid caught at sea, I was posted home on a boat from Bombay. We were diverted to Durban to collect over 1,000 Nazi prisoners of war from New York. When we berthed there the US Army captain who came aboard introduced himself to our chief officer as Captain Beckman. My antennae

77

quivered. Our chief officer said 'You'll like us. We've got a thousand Nazis for you.' 'You should have dumped the bastards overboard,' said the captain.

They chatted for a while. Then, I went over to speak to my name-sake. Yes, he was Jewish. And, yes, there were a few Beckmans scattered about America. But, it was a big place. He could not figure out knowing any Henry Beckman. Perhaps, he said, he changed his name after he left England. That was a strong possibility. I stopped looking. Later, I wondered what I would have greeted him with had I found him; 'Henry Beckman, I presume . . . I'm your cousin from Hackney.'

The 1930s were probably the most dangerous period ever in the history of European Jews. It was like standing at the ocean's edge and becoming aware of the incoming, encircling menacing tide. Even in Hackney Jewish antennae, trained towards Germany, quivered with shock after shock. Mosley had brought something new and evil into England, political anti-semitism, imported direct from his new masters in Nazi Germany. Instead of this individual or that golf club committee disliking Jews a political party, the fascists, were raising support by stoking up hatred against the Jews. Get rid of the Jews and all the ills of the country would disappear. That was the main plank of their manifesto, and it was working. There were more and larger fascist meetings, more gangs of swaggering chanting blackshirts passing through Amhurst Road, more Jews being insulted and pushed around, more daubings on walls and windows and more apprehension among the immigrant generation. Once, they had fled. Where to next?

At the same time there was a strong increase in Jewish nationalism. The inflow of distraught disorientated Jewish refugees fleeing the Nazis added point to the Zionist ideal, a land of our own where Jews could live free from persecution among their own co-religionists. Among friends I made at The

Grocers was Issy Greenstein, brilliantly academic, a quiet but very determined Zionist. When chided about his pipe dream that a Jewish State would come into being he would reply confidently 'We'll get there in the end. We'll be back in Palestine. You just wait and see.'

In 1935 we thrilled to learn that we actually had a Dutch uncle. He was a brother of Mum. His name was Arnold Zwick. He was a large jovial man with a jolly rotund wife, two sons, Leon and Felix, and Feeny a pretty, precocious wide-eyed daughter. The Zwicks manufactured chocolates and toffees.

After the first ice-breaking visit in 1935 they came over every year until the war. They always brought enormous cartons of their confections which, amidst much laughter, Mum and Mary would cart up to Mum's bedroom and hide in the wardrobe. This magnificent made-to-measure piece of furniture had hanging cupboards, shelf sections and long deep drawers. It stretched all the way across the long wall opposite the large double bed. The wood had a rich honey colour and was always being beeswaxed.

The Zwicks stayed at a nearby hotel and came to see us every day. I took Leon and Felix over Hackney Downs where we played football. I took them sight-seeing and although I was a Londoner I thus saw the inside of St. Pauls, Westminster Abbey and Madame Tussauds for the first time. Rose, Freda and Mary took Feeny around London. Their annual visits were eagerly looked forward to. They brought good-humour and much laughter into our household. When the Nazis over-ran Holland we lost contact with the Zwicks.

When Sam was demobilised at the end of 1946 he went to Holland to find out what had happened to them. Thanks to the German penchant for meticulous record keeping and sympathetic help from Red Cross and Dutch officials he found out that Arnold Zwick, his wife and daughter, Feeny, had been transported to Auschwitz, where they were gassed and then burnt in the ovens. Leon Zwick, aged 19, had died of heart failure in a Gestapo prison. Felix Zwick had been in the Dutch Army and had disappeared without trace. Fate, unknown. The grisly search through the mass of records of deaths and deportations to death camps changed Sam. He was very quiet and uncommunicative when he came back.

A poignant post-war recollection were the pages of 'Missing Relatives' advertisements in the *Jewish Chronicle*. They continued for years, gradually diminishing in number until there were no more. Even hope eventually died out.

Chapter Seven

The Cohens acquired a new maid, Maggie. Naturally, she came from the north-east. Her parents were Irish. She was a plain girl with a thin turned-up nose and her brown hair tied back into a bun at the nape of her neck, a fashion in those days. She had the most voluptuous figure ending in very long legs. Wolf whistles from workmen and Maggie went together like fish and chips. She was a cheery extrovert girl with a high octave voice. She frequently came into our garden preceded by her shrieked call sign, 'Mary. I've got something really interesting to tell you.'

When they engaged in conversation Mary listened open-mouthed to Maggie's latest skirmish with the male sex. When Mary came home one evening without Maggie and I asked her why Maggie had not come back with her, out of character she snapped back at me, 'Mind your own business.'

Maggie's figure changed shape. It became noticeable. When I remarked on it Mary said, 'She's getting fat, that's all.' When I observed that it was a funny sort of fatness as it was all in front, Mary replied shortly that people got fat in different ways, then she shooed me out into the garden.

A worried Mrs Cohen came into our house and closeted herself with Mum in the scullery. From behind an open door, not breathing, I listened. Mrs Cohen said that she had advised Maggie to go home, but that was the last thing Maggie wanted to do. She had no desire to see her parents and especially not her father. Innocent days. That puzzled me. Mrs Cohen was at a loss as to what to do. Phil, the medical student, advised Maggie to have an abortion. His advice sent Maggie into an uncontrollable burst of tears. Mr Cohen? He noticed nothing amiss. Maggie and Mary had the most intense conversations at the gap in the wall and then one glorious day an excited Mary rushed back into our kitchen and told Mum that Maggie was getting married.

'To the father?' asked Mum.

'Yes. He's Irish. He owns a pub in Stoke Newington. Next week she's going to stay with him for good.'

Mum exhaled with relief. She slumped down into her arm-hair and said firmly, 'Mary, put on the kettle. Let's have some cake and butter biscuits.'

Mum and Mary were sometimes conspiratorial to the exclusion of everyone else. In Mary, Mum had found a confidante, a comfort, to whom she could speak freely. Mary never let her down and was staunch in seeing that we all helped Mum. When Mum left the house with two empty straw baskets to go shopping in Sandringham Road, Mary would pounce on the nearest male and scold, 'Go on, you lazy lump. Go round and carry your mother's heavy shopping baskets home.' Shamefaced, we always obeyed. Dad, seeing this, once observed that Mary had more feeling in her little finger than all his sons had in their whole bodies. Every morning before he had breakfast Dad went into the dining room to don phylacterics and *tallith* and say his morning prayers. When my brother and I boisterously tried to push one another down the stairs Mary would rush out and tell us to behave ourselves otherwise we would get no breakfast. That always worked. We knew that Mary always meant what she said. Sam dubbed her our Geordie sergeant major.

The mid and late 1930s saw Sam and Mick out most nights at one of the clubs or with girls. Dad, like his contemporaries with adolescent sons, warned us not to consort with non-

Jewish girls. Of course, nature overruled parental strictures and this was probably the most irrevocable dichotomy of all. It resulted in terrible family rows where tempers flared and fathers lost control and even struck their sons. There were gentile girls who confessed that if their parents knew they were going out with Jewish boys they would be in trouble. When these mixed couples were out it was nerve-wracking. They had to keep a weather eye out in case one of the four parents or even someone who would tell their parents spotted them.

Ernie Godwin, a classmate, met a pretty Catholic girl. They became infatuated with one another. Ernie felt that the girl was uncomfortable about something and when he pressed her about it she confessed that her father was a leading light in the British Union of Fascists. Not only that, he was an active speaker at outdoor meetings and Ernie actually saw him speaking at Highbury Corner. When he remarked this to his girlfriend she said that he would murder her if he found out she was going with a Jewish boy. 'Do you share his views?' wondered Ernie, who had not dared to tell his own parents. 'I don't know' she said honestly. 'It's all so confusing. But then you're different.'

How many Jews over the ages have been told that they are different to all the others? How? Taller? Shorter? Better? Worse? More wicked? Meaner? More generous? More honest? Less sly? Dirtier? Cleaner? More this and less that? Hilaire Belloc's unsavoury rhyme 'How odd of God to choose the Jews' had a point. To be the chosen has always been an uneasy burden to bear.

Ernie never really coped with his conflicting emotions. In class he became broody, unable to concentrate on the work. His infatuation, his first, tore him in two. Came the war he went into the navy and the last I heard of him he was serving on a corvette on Atlantic convoy duty.

Pressure of schoolwork increased as I moved into higher

forms, and there was never a day without a good whack of homework. Like Aubrey before me I soon made my mark at my two passions and was opening the batting for my house, Greens, and playing centre forward in the school second XI. Later I moved into the school first XIs at both games. School matches were played Saturday and Wednesday afternoons. The Saturday afternoons were nervous occasions for Aubrey and myself as we sang the Grace After Meals quickly to speed Dad along and then waited for Mum to lure Dad out into the kitchen so that we could grab our packed bags from the chest and race out through the front door.

By the mid-1930s Sam and Mick were old enough to make Dad accept that they would go to synagogue, or not, as it suited them. This left him free to concentrate on Aubrey and myself. We had to go. We were always so bored and impatient during the long services. Fortunately, we had the girls in the gallery to look up at just as they had us to look down at. Dad could never quite accept that his children, lucky enough not to have been in the fearful confines of a Polish ghetto, would inevitably be seduced by the more enjoyable aspects of a tolerant culture. Dad tended to use the Yiddish epithet 'Goy' for gentile. None of us liked it. Once, I dared say to him, 'Why do you use that ugly word, Dad? It's just as bad as Jewboy.' Dad was so affronted I thought he would strike me. But, I was the only one of his children who showed interest in his past and now and again he opened out to me. So, he explained quietly:

> I can only talk from what I have experienced. Like us, there are good goys and bad ones. I work with them. I live among them. Some are honest. Some are not. But, if the blackshirts increase many times, and it could happen, not just the odd Jew will get beaten up. They'll be hauling us out of our houses and killing us . . . All right. Maybe you'll never see a Russian progrom in Hackney. But why

should we always have to live under the threat just because we are Jewish? Answer me that. Your friend Issy has the right idea. We need our own country. That is the only solution. But it's a pipe dream. It can never happen . . . never.

The steady flow of refugees from Nazi terror kept on coming. Families took them in. Clubs gave them shelter and beds to sleep in, sleeping bags, use of showers and toilets and even food. The surge of generosity by East End Jews towards the refugees was spontaneous. No one held back. More frequently as the 1930s headed towards war Dad would bring back refugees for a Friday night dinner. Once, he brought home a German couple.

They were obviously top of the tree people. He explained that he was a physicist who lectured at universities. His wife was a teacher. They admitted to being the least observant of Jews. Before the Nazis they had regarded themselves as being German, and that was that. They politely declined Dad's invitation to take them to the Sabbath morning synagogue service but did accept the invitation to Saturday lunch. They both spoke very passable English and the lunch went well. At the end I went out into the garden. The physicist came out to join me. We small-talked pleasantly, then he handed me a small hard leather case, and said, 'I'm sorry we are in no position to return your family's hospitality so would you accept the gift as a token of our thanks.' The case held a medal. He told me it was the iron cross, first class, and that he had won it while fighting against the English on the western front in 1917. At that moment Rose appeared. She took the medal and handed it back to the physicist, telling him that we were delighted to have him for a meal anytime but that we could not really take anything in return. He was taken aback. I was miffed. Later Rose said, 'The fact that he has brought it with him shows that he treasures it. Also, it is no longer a German medal. It's a Nazi one. If Dad saw it he would take a hammer and pound it into junk.'

Probably because of the rising threat of fascism I commenced to take a deeper interest in Jewish history. I began to read about the early Jewish Zionist visionaries and I drew great pride in the early pioneers who slaved and died as they drained malarial swamps and irrigated desert land in Palestine, idealism their only motive. It was easy for Issy and another friend, Berl, to persuade me to join a Zionist youth movement called *Habonim* (The builders).

Habonim was conceived in 1928 when Chaim Weizmann, the Zionist leader, brought a Zionist worker from Tel Aviv to London. His name was Wellesley Aron and his task was to see what could be done about British Jewish youth. A Charles Rubens took him on a tour of the Jewish boys clubs; Cambridge, Brady, Bethnal Green, Hackney, West Central and my own favourite, Stamford Hill. Aron was dismayed to find that they were wholly sports and social centres. Rubens charged Aron with getting them interested in Jewish history and culture. Aron conceived of the idea of the Jewish equivalent of the Scout movement with culture and history thrown in.

One Sunday evening he gave his first lecture entitled 'How to bring Palestine and Jewish culture to English-speaking Jews'. He spoke at 77 Great Russell Street, headquarters of the Zionist Organisation. It was a very inclement November evening. Only six people turned up.

Aron was so depressed he determined to bother no more. But, one of his audience, a South African named Norman Lourie begged him to repeat the talk. Aron did so the following week. To his amazement the hall was packed. Lourie was in the chair. He proposed that Aron should proceed with his ideals and the proposal was overwhelmingly passed.

Aron struggled against apathy and lack of interest. But, he was a dogged individual, determined to build up the movement. He devised a *Habonim* uniform of navy stockings, khaki shorts and a blue shirt with a breast pocket badge depicting a pioneer under a palm holding a spade and a rifle. He created an acceptance test which consisted mainly of knowledge of Jewish history. He wrote the *Habonim* handbook. This laid down *Habonim* ideals and how the movement would be run.

He was then acting as Permanent Secretary of the Zionist Organisation, a paid post enabling him to stay on in London. One Friday he was told that he was not needed at the weekly executive meeting so he sneaked into the vacant offices of Weizmann, Professor Brodetsky, Sokoloff and Arlozorff and left his handbook on their desks for them to read. After they had left the building he returned to their offices and hit his lowest point. The handbooks had been dumped into waste-paper baskets, obviously unread.

But Aron was a resilient character. Despite indifference, by the early 1930s *Habonim* was taking root. Most parents were antagonistic towards the movement. They did not understand it. They did not want it to distract their offspring from scrambling up the prosperity ladder and they were most certainly against them rushing off to drain the fever swamps in Palestine.

Aron suddenly realised that he had found an unwanted but unexpected ally. The clarification of Nazi intentions towards the Jews was beginning to turn the minds of Jewish youth in various countries towards the creation of a Jewish National Home. Great Russell Street noticed a marked increase in the number of boys and girls applying to join *Habonim*. One die had become cast. There would be no Jewish National Home in places like Uganda or the fringes of the Sahara desert. It would be the Holy Land or bust.

In 1932 Aron and his wife and child returned to Tel Aviv and Joe Gilbert, an energetic Londoner, took over the running of the movement. He gave it direction and a refreshing sense of purpose. The end purpose, he declared, was the creation of a Jewish State in Palestine. So, let us go for it. The message was powerful in its simplicity. It lit fires in young boys and girls and some went to work on farms and to study at agricultural colleges with a view to making themselves useful on *kibbutzim* in Palestine.

A boy named Max Addess had moved into our circle of friends. At first, I found him lugubrious yet comical with it. He would do things while saying at the same time that he did not know why he was doing it. Issy brought Max along to join *Habonim*. I had soon found a warmth and unity of purpose and enjoyed being called *chaver* (comrade). It was not in the communist sense of the term. Walls were covered by maps of the land of Israel, coloured in blue, photographs of early pioneers and portraits of Zionist founders and leaders. Dad was very upset at my having joined *Habonim* and he complained

> You go to Stamford Hill and other boys clubs and you're always playing football over Hackney Downs and you're always rushing through your homework far too quickly to learn from it. Your reports say you can do better if you work harder. Don't you want to make something of yourself?

The fissure between us widened a little further.

One day I acquired a companion who insisted upon accompanying me right into the school and who would only slink home when gruffly admonished by one of the masters. She was a black bitch, half retriever and half various other breeds. We called her Gipsy. She had an alert perky face with black soulful eyes, especially appealing when she wanted to go out with you, or saw you eating. She attached herself to me. When I was in the bathroom she would wait outside and then bound all over me when I emerged. When I went to school she stalked just behind me. My commands of 'Naughty dog. Go home' would halt her. But when I turned around again there she was, maintaining position like a ship in convoy. And, there she would stay with me right across the wide school playground to the imposing school entrance until one of the masters sent her packing.

Gipsy slept in a large wicker basket in the kitchen, furnished with straw and two large cushions. Nearby was her water bowl and a large enamelled plate always filled with bones and biscuits. Her Heaven was to grip a large meaty bone between her front paws and nibble it right down to extinction.

Gipsy always accompanied Mum to Schlagman the butcher and she was never disappointed. With all the histrionics of a stage magician he would produce an enormous bone with meaty knuckles at both ends. The looks she gave Schlagman at those moments were ones of sheer love. When she walked home alongside Mum with the bone gripped tightly between slavering jaws she growled unmistakeable warnings to dogs which approached to investigate the bone with blatantly felonious intent.

Gipsy soon learned to sneak out on her own and visit Schlagman. He never let her down. He gave her tit-bits of meat to eat on the spot and a large bone to take home. I often took her over Hackney Downs and threw bouncy sorbo balls for her to chase and it was while doing this that she gave me my most embarrassing experience to date.

It was mating time, which my innocence in such matters overlooked. She was sniffing around with a prancing excite-able Airedale dog I threw the ball. Gipsy chased it. Her new friend chased after Gipsy. They did not return. Both dogs ignored my shouts and disappeared from view. I gave up and engaged in a game of football. When I returned home an hour later, there was no Gipsy. Mary chased me back to Hackney Downs to find her and her randy companion. He had had his way with her. They were both shaggily haired at the back and were stuck together, backside to backside. They were encircled by an amused crowd of men, women and schoolgirls. A man and a woman were each pulling a dog, trying to part them.

Gipsy saw me and went berserk with relief. She tugged the Airedale towards me. It howled with pain. My instinct was to turn and flee but her imploring eyes rendered flight impossible. The schoolgirls were having a field day, their anatomical comments making my face burn. I grabbed Gipsy's shoulder and pulled gently. No good. The advice came thick and fast.

'That won't do it. Give a hard quick tug, mate.'

'Get a scissors and cut the hairs.'

'Daft ha'peth' scorned a woman. 'He's a schoolboy. Where would he get a scissors from?'

I was advised to keep Gipsy inside until the heat was off, to get her doctored, to sprinkle pepper on her bottom and to feed her with some type of pills. Men took it in turns to grab the other dog and pull at which both dogs howled in pain. Finally, a man emerged from a nearby house with a bucket of very warm water. He told everyone to stand back and then he carefully emptied the water over the two canine bottoms. It worked. Gipsy, in her joy, jumped up to lick my face.

'Bad dog' I swore at her and as I walked away very very fast, she bounded all around jumping up to lick my face. 'Bad wicked dog.'

I kept the incident to myself. Anxiously, I watched Gipsy closely for tell-tale signs of pregnancy, but nothing happened. Dad tolerated Gipsy, provided she was where he was not. Mary spoiled her with snacks, unable to resist her Bisto kid looks. Mum enjoyed having Gipsy lying at her feet while she mended and Gipsy carried on her personal war against the cats who ventured into our garden. After she had chased a cat back into the builders' yard she would leap up at the high wall at the back barking triumphantly. Once, however, an enormous bruiser of a feral ginger cat came striding down our garden path towards the house. Gipsy rushed out at her, barking wildly. Instead of fleeing the enormous cat stood its ground. It arched its muscular back and hissed so balefully at Gipsy that she skidded to a halt. Barking half-heartedly, she retreated backwards at ever increasing speed into the house. 'Never mind, pet,' laughed Mary. 'I wouldn't like to tangle with that cat myself.' She patted Gipsy to soothe her ruffled pride.

For two years Gipsy became part of the family. Even Dad, when he thought he was unobserved, patted her head and talked to her. Gipsy instinctively stayed clear of him when he was eating or praying. She accompanied Mum to the shops and very quickly learned to wheedle biscuits from Debbie Samuels and from the Maisies.

One morning while I was in the bathroom I realised something was different. There was no Gipsy whining and scratching at the door. I went downstairs and passed Aubrey on the up. Instead of the usual friendly shoulder charge and scuffle he just hurried past me. I sat down in the kitchen for breakfast. No Gipsy. Mary was making a tremendous clatter in the scullery. 'Where's Gipsy?' I called out again. No answer from Mary. Then, Mick appeared. He sat down opposite and said 'I'll give it to you straight. She's dead. She was hit by a passing car. The driver didn't stop.'

'Oh . . . .' Breakfast was left untouched. 'Where is she?'

'Outside, lying in the gutter. But . . . don't go. There's nothing you can do . . .'

Mick tried to hold me back. I struggled free with Mary yelling at Mick to let me go. Outside there was the warm promise of a summer's day to come. Sacking had been thrown over Gipsy. I went to pull it aside, squeamish as to what I would see. Rose came up behind me, put her arms around me and hugged me sympathetically. She eased me back into the house. All that day it was a household bereft. Mary cried, Mum was visibly upset and when Dad came home and was told the news he was shocked. The Cohens came in and commiserated. That day at school I heard nothing and learned less. The dustcart took Gipsy away in a sack. It took many weeks for the loss to become bearable. Dad refused point blank to have another dog. He said it was too painful to lose them.

In the centre of the school building was the Dome, so called because a dome completely surmounted the large amphitheatre that could seat up to 800 boys. A stage formed one segment of the circle at ground level. To both sides of it tier after tier of wooden seating rose backwards and upwards to a circle of stained glass windows. Topping these windows was the dome. At the end of every term the entire school assembled in the Dome to listen to the headmaster's report. On these occasions boys who had achieved great things academically, in the arts and in sport would be singled out for praise and applause. I never made it scholastically but . . .

One warm June afternoon The Grocers first XI played Monoux school at cricket. We batted first. I opened with a boy named Saville, always neat and precise in dress and in whatever he did.

I took the first strike. It was one of those rare occasions when the ball seemed so large and my timing felt so precision perfect that I could hit the ball anytime, anywhere, anyhow. School matches were played in the afternoons. Both sides had to bat and scores of 40 and 50 were regarded as being very good. I hit the first over for three fours. As I started, I kept going. I hit several sixes, hooking the ball onto a sloping, tiled school roof. I hit the clock and stopped it and damaged several roof tiles. I just kept going my merry way as wickets tumbled at the other end and then I heard my team mates calling out and clapping. I had scored 102 not out, the first boy to have scored a century in a school match. At the assembly at term's end my feat was read out by the headmaster and I was lustily cheered by the school. Sporting achievements always did get the greatest ovations. Philistinism ruled okay.

The masters at The Grocers were professional to their fingertips. When they entered a classroom with their black gowns swishing behind them they commanded respect by taking it for granted that it was their due. Outside of school there was no fraternisation between boys and masters. Absenteeism was closely queried. Truancy was non-existent, and they could make up boys' minds. French was compulsory and then it was a choice between learning Latin or German. I pondered over this until my form master called me over to him and said,

'Well, Beckman, have you made up your mind? German or Latin?'

'Mmm . . .' I had no idea which to go for. 'Mmm . . .'

'Enough mmms.' The master shut me up and said 'Will you go into law?' I shook my head. 'Medicine?' I shook my head. 'No point in going in for a language which will be no earthly use to you. You'll learn German. That's settled, then?'

'Yessir.'

My first German teacher was a Mr Buckey, a fresh-faced man with thinning hair and neat thin moustachio. He had been captured leading a night patrol on the western front and had taken the pains to learn German thoroughly while a prisoner of war. He could be irascible, sarcastic and impatient with pupils who fell behind. He said they held up his schedule. German grammar and sentence construction gave the most trouble. Those of us who grasped it would be waylaid by less fortunate boys after school. Generally, we helped. It was said that Buckey admired the Nazis. If so, he never showed signs of it.

Later we passed into the hands of a German exchange teacher. He came from Düsseldorf. He was in his late twenties, with thick brushed-back blonde hair, china blue eyes and a thin fish-hook mouth. He smiled a lot. I was one of six Jewish boys in his class. None of us doubted that he was a dyed-in-the-wool Nazi. Although he did watch his behaviour he could never conceal his pride at Nazi successes. When the Germans annexed the Sudetenland and then Czechoslovakia he was as buoyant as a kite in a gale. He taught us well. Even though the Jewish boys, because of the Yiddish they had grown up with, could grasp German more speedily than the others, there was an underlying bad feeling between us. It was a treading on eggshell situation.

He was instrumental in arranging an exchange visit between The Grocers and the Oberrealschule of Soest, Westphalia. No Jewish boy went with the school party to Germany. From our boys who went over there we learned that the German boys were already becoming trained soldiers. They went to training camp and learned field craft and how to handle all types of weapons. When the German boys shepherded by two teachers returned the visit the stresses and strains broke out everywhere.

Apart from their sight-seeing, contests were arranged between the two schools in every type of sport and athletics, cricket excepted. And, herein entered the problems. A sprinkling of Jewish boys represented the school in most activities and this threw us into a deep spin. What should we do? Participate, or not? Whereas our gentile schoolmates called them Germans, to us they were Nazis. Our loyalty to the school was very strong. We did not want to let the school down and make it easier for the visitors to win at anything. Nevertheless, opinion came down against participation. Our teachers were aware of the ferment. So was our German teacher. Still, he had arranged the exchange successfully and was like a dog with two tails. One morning he buttonholed me in the playground. He was amiability itself as he said,

'Ah, Beckman. You will be playing in the football match against Soest next Wednesday afternoon? Yes?'

'I don't know' I replied. He was the only master I did not call 'sir'. Nor did other Jewish boys. He could have reported us for lack of respect, a punishable offence, but he never did. He knew that the inhumanities being perpetrated by his countrymen against Continental Jews could not be smiled away. He said,

'I've been telling our boys what a good team you have.'

'I see. Well, if you please excuse me. I must go . . . .'

The one other Jewish boy in the team, Sheinman, a stocky hard-tackling right half back, and I had decided not to play. Then, Mr Day, our sports master grabbed us. He did not beat about the bush. He said very firmly 'Now, listen you two. I am aware of your feelings. Having said that you still owe loyalty to the school and your team mates. We want to field our best team and win. You want that as well, don't you?'

We could only reply 'Yessir.'

'Good' said Mr Day. 'That's settled. You'll both play.' He added emphatically 'That is an order.'

Free expression in schools did not then exist. Masters gave orders, pupils jumped to obey. The game was played over Hackney Downs on a gravel pitch. Their players were much taller than we were. They wore blue stockings, blue shorts and white jerseys. On their left breasts were their school badges. Lower, to the right, each jersey sported a small red swastika nestling inside a black circle. Sheinman sidled over to me and said 'See those swastikas. I'm glad I'm playing, now. Let's get stuck into the sods.'

We did. In truth, football was not their metier. We went past them, through them and underneath them with the sliding tackles that were banned in the inter-house matches played on those gravel pitches. We bloodied many German knees and we won by ten goals to nil. It was so one-sided that the master refereeing the game urged us to ease up. He penalised us for being offside, when we were not, and disallowed two or three goals. But, ignited by the tigerishness of Sheinman and myself, all the team played flat out. Our goalkeeper was reduced to coming up to the halfway line and calling out plaintively 'Pass it back. Give me a kick.' When the final whistle went the Germans clapped politely. Some boys exchanged handshakes. Sheinman and I hurried to the touchline and collected our bags and clothing. The next day the German teacher said to me,

'Congratulations. You played well.'

'Thanks.'

'You taught our boys a lesson.'

'At football, yes.'

The school orchestra ran into similar turbulence. About one third of the musicians were Jewish. They decided to boycott the concert to be played in honour of our German guests. The music teacher thought otherwise. Aided by heavy albeit discreet assistance from the headmaster he won the day. He was born British. Both his parents were Italian. He had a sardonic sense of humour. The music played contained much Mahler and Mendelssohn.

The boxing tournament. Three out of the eight weights were represented by Jewish boys. Two of them suffered the same conflict of conscience but succumbed to the inevitable pressure and boxed. A contrary attitude was taken by our heavyweight champion, Alex Schwarz. 'Not fight the buggers?' he exclaimed. 'I'm bloody looking forward to it.'

The contest took place in the gymnasium before a packed house which included all the German party, boys and guest adults. Mr Marley, the gym master, with a beer belly pushing the stretch of his singlet to its limits, umpired the bouts. He had been a regimental sergeant major during the war and was a rough and ready character who stood no nonsense. He was a hard compact man behind his beer belly. He had a booming voice and his teaching was effectively primitive. For example, his method of teaching boys to swim was to line them up on the edge of the swimming pool and walk down the line, pushing them in. He did that to me. I was at the deep end and gazing down apprehensively at the green chlorinated waters, when a hard fist in my back propelled me into them. I went under, surfaced, swallowed water, went under again and was threshing about in a panic when a boy grabbed me and pulled me into the side. As I hung onto the rail running under the lip of the bath, retching and spluttering, Marley's flushed, moustachioed face bent over mine and he snarled 'Next time you go into the water keep your bloody mouth shut. That's lesson one.'

At track events, discus, putting the shot and throwing the javelin the German boys came out on top. At swimming and diving, football and boxing, they never stood a chance. The seven hors d'oeuvres bouts went our way and then everyone hushed for the eighth and biggest, the heavyweight contest involving Alex Schwarz. Alex was a natural who could put together a flurry of punches with telling effect. He won his inter-school bouts with ease and went on to box for a top club in the Amateur British Boxing Association competitions. What made anticipation of his fight electric was his expressed and undisguised relish at getting a hated Nazi in his sights. He made no bones about his intention to make a meal of it. Everyone in that gymnasium knew that Alex was Jewish, even the Germans.

His opponent was a tall willowy boy, well muscled around the shoulders and arms. He wore the Soest school's white singlet with its swastika badge. Alex stared at it with great intensity. Within a minute of the first round having started Alex was in complete control. He had the German down twice. He bloodied his nose and it was obvious he could have ended the fight in that first round. But, he eased up. At the bell Mr Day went over to his corner and spoke to him. Alex shook his head. Mr Day looked angry.

Alex toyed with the German in the second round. The German just managed to totter back to his stool when the bell went. A grim Mr Day went across to speak to Marley. Marley shook his head. He was the umpire. The boxing ring was his domain and the best way to get Mr Marley not to do something was to tell him to do it. Alex picked his opponent off at will, cut him just below his left eye and split his lip until, with seconds to go, he unleashed a powerful punch to the German's temple and knocked him out.

The Grocers schoolboys all cheered. Our German teacher

sat, po-faced. Mr Day looked very angry. The German party of two masters and boys sat very quietly. Marley, quite unnecessarily, raised Alec's arm high in victory.

It was a relief to everyone when the Soest boys went home. They were polite and behaved well, but there was a marked lack of warmth on both sides. One thing stood out. They were well on the way to being trained soldiers. If anything sign-posted that war was on the way, they did. About five months before Germany invaded Poland our German teacher went home. It was rumoured that his contract had not expired. One day, he was with us and the next, he was gone.

1 Sam, Barney and Nat Beckman,
first cousins

2 George Clarfelt

3 Sister Freda and her husband Hymie

4 Sister Rose and husband
Harry Lavy

5 Photograph taken circa 1910
Top line: Aunt Tamara,
Aunt Golda, author's mother
Bottom line: Aunt Rose,
maternal grandmother,
Aunt Hannah

6 Author and brother Michael

7 Rosamund who married
brother Sam

8 Brother Sam, infantry, 8th army

9 Brother Aubrey, RAF

10 Author's mother

11 Author

12 Max Addess during pilot
training

13 Norman Myers, RAF

14 Maccabi team at Stade Lenin before match against French football champions (amateur) in Paris

15 Author and his wife, Patricia, in Brighton, August 1948

17 Hackney Downs School Football First XI, 1936–7 season

Chapter Eight

My Barmitzvah. A second before midnight on 21 February 1934 I was still a boy. A second after that same midnight Jewish tradition metamorphosised me into a man. The change in my status produced immediate results. The short trousers which exposed my chapped knees to the cold winter winds gave way to long trousers. Every day Dad made me don phylacteries and *tallit* and pray in the dining room before I went to school. I endured the unctuous observations that I was now a man and Dad actually treated me like an adult.

We established a new rapport helped by the fact that I was his only child who nagged him to speak about his early days in The Pale. I learned that his father, my grandfather who I never saw, had been a carpenter and a Talmudic scholar. How there were times when he dared not stray outside the ghetto boundaries because of the irrational abuse and flash violence that could erupt against Jews. How Utopian for East European Jews was that fabulous land way across the seas, America. And how one day he and another boy trekked across Europe to Hamburg to travel steerage to America. How the ship berthed in London, had engine trouble and how he was befriended by a Jewish fishmonger off Brick Lane and thus he stayed in England.

Now, after my barmitzvah, I walked to shul alongside him and we held adult conversations. Now that technically I was a man, I gratified Dad by being honoured to perform services like opening and closing the ark and being called upon to carry the scrolls of the law around the synagogue before and after the appropriate portion of the law was read out.

Four months before my actual Barmitzvah Dad brought home a rabbi to teach me to master the words and the notes of the portion of law that I would have to chant during my synagogue ordeal. It was '*Kee Seessoh*', the longest portion of the year. I cursed my bad luck. The rabbi came two evenings a week for hourly lessons. The evenings when he came, added to school homework, gave me no time to go out and play and made me very mutinous. Mary kept an eagle eye on me when the rabbi was due and would say 'You're going to learn it properly and make your father proud of you. He deserves that. Besides' she said once, 'I'll be there to see you do it.'

'You? In synagogue? Dad will go mad . . .'

'Forget I said that' said Mary hastily. 'Your sisters and Bessie Cohen said they will take me in with them.'

When the great day came and I chanted my piece on the *bima* at Shacklewell Lane Synagogue I looked up at Mary in the gallery. She was sitting between Freda and Rose. A wide-brimmed hat concealed her face. She raised her hand and gave me a surruptitious wave. That was the only point where I stumbled in the performance. Yet, the aficionados of Barmitzvah performances noticed it. Dad wondered why I had lost concentration and spoiled a clean sheet with that one blemish. Mary was so much part of the family that it seemed right that she be there.

The rabbi who taught me came from Poland. He was a sad man, dull and humourless, a reflection of his lifestyle. He suffered from halitosis which forced me to feign a severe cold and keep a handkerchief pressed against my nose. He had a pallid complexion, china blue eyes and a scrawny mottled beard. He always wore the same black serge suit, shiny with age and wear. The cuffs were frayed and he wore it every time he saw me. His chosen vocation was certainly not making him rich and, looking back, he must have been struggling to keep his head above water. He was patient. He never showed emotion. His persistence made me tone and word perfect.

The last time he came, Dad entered the dining room and without saying a word sat down quietly in an armchair and listened to me go through the whole portion without a mistake. He nodded with satisfaction and went out quietly. I often wondered how much my Barmitzvah cost him, adding yet another burden to his overstrained financial back.

A feature of Jewish households in the 1930s was the accumulation of collecting boxes lined up on kitchen mantelpieces. There were over 20 on ours; for religious organisations, for Zionist groups, for charities of all types, for institutions. The most prominent was the fabled blue and white Jewish National Fund box. Then, every Jewish office, shop, factory and home had one. It was the box that most selected to put their loose change into. There is no doubt that the silver and copper put into these boxes and used to buy land in Palestine for the settlers made an emphatic contribution towards changing the history of the Middle East.

The boxes begat collectors, woebegone, down at heel men. Their expressions never failed to make Dad add more coins to a collecting box when they expressed reproach at its lack of weight. All the boxes supported worthy causes and Dad would give when he could ill afford it. The worthiest cause of all was protecting Dad from his greatest weakness, an inability to say no. Mum feared to interfere with Dad's generosity, but Rose could be a tigress. When she spotted Dad coming back from the open street door to get more coins she would rush to it and firmly tell the collector to beat it. If they hung about waiting for Dad's return Rose would shut the door in their faces.

Most mornings when I went to school I turned left on leaving the house, encountering lots of schoolmates on the way. Occasionally, for a change of scene, I turned right and then after a few minutes I turned left into Anton Street, about 100 yards long. One side had a row of neat terraced houses and the other side was home to a great local institution, the Star laundry. Its large fleet of natty yellow and chocolate delivery vans would be lined up on both sides of the street. Their drivers in matching chocolate coats and yellow caps queued to place their vehicles alongside the wide despatch platform where two chains of men and women loaded them up with neatly parcelled bundles for delivery. During the daytime these cheerful busy vans could be seen buzzing about everywhere, delivering and collecting. They were as much part of the Hackney scene as the red buses and corporation utility carts.

The bottom end of Anton Street formed a T-junction with the railway arches, above which ran the London and North Eastern railway. The British Union of Fascists successfully concealed records and documents in one of those arches throughout the war. Most of the arches were rented out to one or two-man businesses. They nearly all dealt in cars. From early morning the narrow street would be littered with car engines in pieces, cars being stripped, sprayed, repaired, panel beaten, bought and sold. Every workshop had its mangy mean-looking alsatian dog. Overnight these dogs were locked up in the premises with food and water. If one dog was disturbed it set off a cacophony of barking that could be heard a long way away. There were no burglaries in those arches. During the day the dogs were allowed to run freely and rummage through the debris. Running the gauntlet of them was a good test of one's nerve. Between two of the arches there was a gateway leading into the back playground of the school.

Everything about The Grocers was competitive. It was normal. We had strenuous mid-term tests. These showed up weaknesses which boys then strove to strengthen for the serious end of term examinations. The school was its teachers. They varied. I remember two, especially, one for the right reason and the other for his mild sadism.

There was Mr Swan who taught mathematics. He wore the almost uniform dark suit with white shirt and regimental tie. His rectangular spectacles with tortoiseshell rims gave him a benign look, despite severe short, iron grey hair. He was casual, laid back and humorous. But, how he could get knowledge into boys.

He would perch on the side of his desk tapping the blackboard with a very long cane, which he never used on boys, and just talked to us as if it were a fireside chat. He made everything so logical and simple. He never put a boy on punishment. He never had to, we were always so rapt on whatever he was saying. He would say:

> Maths is the easiest subject to master. You can make mistakes in other subjects but in maths the figures won't let you. They are totally logical. Two plus two can only equal four. Nothing else. Don't be frightened by maths. It hasn't killed anyone, yet [a slow grin] . . . as far as I know, of course.

As he chatted away, we learned. He gave little homework. The last lesson of the day, when he taught us, he would stay on for a while to help puzzled boys. He shepherded his duller pupils through examinations and anyone with the slightest aptitude into winning honours and distinctions.

There were teachers who were interested and others who made learning hard work. There were very few who made learning so boring that we only looked forward to the end of the lessons. We appreciated teachers who stayed behind and patiently answered questions. There were those who gathered up their papers and fled the moment they heard the bell. There were those we liked and those we disliked. We hated Mr Dellfield, a low-key sadist.

He was a large pulpy man with thick fingers and a jowly face with thick lips. He was tonsurally bald. He never showed emotion and taught his subject, history, without enthusiasm. The repeal of the corn laws and Nelson's famous victory at Trafalgar emerged with the same sausage-machine monotone.

He would set us work, tell us to get on with it and move to the back of the classroom. He would warn us to keep our heads down over our work and that if we turned our heads we would be punished with 200 lines. Quietly, he would move slowly down the rows of desks and suddenly tweak a boy's ear hard, admonishing 'You're not concentrating' or 'You've blotted your work'. As a variation he would carry a 12-inch wooden ruler and hit boys with its edge, or jab them with it in the small of their backs. Hard. His most unnerving trick was to stand for a long time behind a boy who stiffened in antici-pation of a painful tweak, or cuff or painful jab. This was the worst torture of all. No boy reported him. Yet, we all did reasonably well in history. It was a subject you could do reason-ably well in if you worked hard enough at it.

What with school, sports, the boys clubs and *Habonim* life was very full. Of course, there were always the fascists. Molestation, being pushed off pavements and verbal abuse was standard enough to live with. When in 1936 a gang of them threw an elderly Jewish couple through a plate glass window in Kingsland High Road a frisson of déjà vu afflicted the elderly immigrants and those refugees from German Nazism. To add spice the more adventurous of us would set out after dark to stalk the roaming gangs of blackshirts. Fights did occur. Boys who produced trophies of fascist caps or swastika armbands were greatly admired. Boys who limped home with undisguisable battered faces faced the wrath of their parents. Dad would tear into me, saying 'It's not clever to be out late at night by yourself. Those swine are always looking for trouble . . .'

'Don't worry,' I assured him. 'I always keep my eyes peeled. I'll avoid them.' Once, however, I was careless.

I had been to the Stamford Hill club rehearsing for a concert.

My enthusiasm outweighed my talent and I helped make up a chorus line. It was great fun. About 10.30 p.m. three of us left the club and walked down Amhurst Park to the major crossing by the Regent cinema. Max, who had been busily predicting what a shambles the whole concert would be on the night, turned off to Egerton Road where he lived near the synagogue. Instead of turning right down towards Stoke Newington High Street, the shorter way home, I accompanied Danny down to the Clapton ponds. Thence, I decided to short cut across Hackney Downs. Those days we walked everywhere. The aristocrats owned bicycles. It was a fine evening. Utterly relaxed I strode down Kenninghall Road and entered the Downs. I walked under the foliage, put up by the two rows of the magnificent oaks that ringed the perimeter of the Downs, and cut down an asphalt pathway towards home.

Hackney Downs resembled in shape a squashed circle. Its hub was a rest area, circular, its perimeter ringed by more oaks and sycamores. At its centre was a water fountain set in granite stone. From this centre paths radiated like spokes of a wheel out to the edges of the Downs. I walked down the path leading to the exit in Downs Park Road by the LNER bridge. I think my mind was on cricket, the concert and the pretty soloist with whom I had exchanged encouraging glances. Before I realised it four young blackshirts in their full Nazi uniforms, on a high, smelling of beer, were onto me. The one before me raised his hand and pushed my chest, gloating 'That's as far as you go, Jewboy.'

Two of the others were moving each side to get behind me. Then, and I never knew how I managed it, the adrenalin of shock and fear galvanised me into swinging round and hitting the one on my left on his face and, at the same time, jumping from a standing start clean over the four feet high railing. My shoe hit the top railing, making me land on hands and knees. Scrabbling frantically to my feet I hared it back the way I'd come through the long grass.

They came after me, yelling what they would do to the fucking Jewboy. Perceiving that I wanted to get down through the railway arches into Amhurst Road they spread out in a curving line, forcing me to run back to where I had entered the Downs. I ran along the north side of the Downs and then headed back down the slope leading to the railway line. I noticed that two of them had fallen away behind. The other two were trotting easily across a large field to cut off my way back to the arches. I paused to take stock. I noticed the field leading down to the archway I had my eye on actually steepened considerably down towards the railway. I felt so hyped up I could have flown. I decided to go for it. I hurtled down the field, feeling myself running faster and faster. I passed the nearest fascist with yards to spare. I hurdled the last railing and was then under the arch, stumbling on large stones and half bricks. It was pitch black inside that archway. But looking out I could see clearly the silhouette of the fascist who had kept up with me. He had stopped, puzzled. He could not see me. I bent down and picked up a chunky piece of brick. The fascist was uncertain, irresolute and by himself. I took a long calming breath and then rushed out at him, shouting 'Right, you bastard, We're one to one . . .'

He saw me raise my arm and realised I was clutching a missile to throw at him. He looked back and saw that his nearest comrade was quite a distance away. He turned and ran back up the slope. I chased him, got very close and threw the brick. Through cricket I had developed a long hard throw. The brick hit his shoulder with great force. He yelled, and stumbled onto all fours. Two of his comrades were coming up at a fast lick. I scooted back up a narrow short alley into Amhurst Road. No one was about. I raced across the road and dived into one of the large bush and plant filled front gardens of one of those detached houses opposite. Later, these spacious mansions were demolished to make way for Lewis Trust dwellings. By front garden and front garden I made my way towards home. When I reached the last house, before having to traverse the open Downs Park Road, I stood behind a tree and saw the four fascists emerge from the alley into Amhurst Road. They looked left and right. One was clutching his shoulder and seemed to be in some discomfort. Then, they disappeared back into the alley.

I walked home. I suffered an insatiable thirst. In the scullery I drank two large tumblers of cold water. It was cold and delicious. Then, there was no such thing as bottled water. Mary was sitting quietly, reading a book. She looked up, 'You look guilty. What have you been up to?'

'Rehearsing at the club. It just went on and on . . .'

'Howie,' she scoffed. 'I believe you but thousands wouldn't.'

Of course there were always rumours and reports of incidents between blackshirts and Jews. A particular nasty blackshirt sport was targeting. This happened well after dark on late night buses, usually around the Dalston Junction area. Fascists would watch a Jew get onto a bus. As it moved off they rushed to jump aboard it, beat up their victim and jumped off it quickly. Strangely, they became part of the fabric of daily life. More disquieting to the imaginative was the non-stop flow of shocked penurious Jewish refugees from the Nazis. British Jews pulled out all the stops to help them, but they kept on arriving.

The news from Europe was all bad. It reached the stage where Dad would pick up a newspaper, glance at it and then throw it down, saying that he could not bear to read it. Attitudes changed. More trenchant sermons from the pulpits began to harp on the need for a Jewish National Home. The dreaded question 'Could it happen here?' surfaced and aroused intense arguments. There were those who said of course not. There were the prevaricators who said that it could only happen if Mosley got into power but that would never happen in a democratic country like Britain. The holders of a third opinion were few, mainly young and growing in number. They did not want to be tolerated anywhere. They were developing a steely determination to go for a Jewish State. Issy was one of these.

With so few exceptions as to be discountable the immigrant generation of Jewish women never worked after they married. Their hands were filled with the raising and looking after the needs of large families. Like the others Mum was too tired to be anything but compliant to Dad's wish and word. Yet, when she felt occasion demanded, she could exhibit a courage and steadfastness that balked Dad. This usually happened when she saved one of her sons from a beating which she felt was not deserved. Dad's explosive temper could make him unaware of what he was doing. Thus, when he really blew his top and reached for his leather belt the errant son would race for the sycamore at the back of the garden and climb up it for safety. Dad would stand at the foot of the tree and order his son to climb down at once. It was a ritual. The son up the tree would wait for Mum to come into the garden, which she always did, and she refused to leave Dad until he gave her the belt, which he always did. When he was incandescent with rage, he was dangerous. In cold blood he could not hit anyone.

Dad would never give way on anything that touched on Judaic religion and custom. If it meant so much more work to have separate cutlery and crockery for meat and milk, and a complete changeover for separate sets for Passover, used for one week a year, so it had to be.

Chapter Nine

Haskel. Dad had a habit of bringing home the odd lame duck for a good square Friday night meal. Mum never complained or turned a hair. She just served up smaller portions. Only Aubrey, as thin as a rake and always ravenous, grumbled that this was carrying hospitality a bit too far. He ate more than anyone else and would finish what others left on their plates. Anyone or anything depriving Aubrey of food was a threat.

Usually the strays made one appearance. But Haskel became the exception, a frequent guest and then a part of the family scene. At first, he sat by himself at a small table in the kitchen, unshaven, unkempt and wearing his ankle-length black over-coat, shiny with grease and embedded dirt. Most off-putting was his smell, the odour of poverty and the hostel he slept in. No one referred to it. We felt a bit ashamed that he did not eat with us but it was his sour odour that put us off. Nevertheless, he always enjoyed his meal and before leaving would take Mum's hand and kiss it and say 'That was very good, Mrs Beckman. God will bless you.'

It was a bitterly cold morning when a pinched shivering Haskel wandered into Dad's shop and asked for work. Dad had none to offer but, being Dad, offered him some money. To his surprise Haskel refused, declaring angrily that he was not a beggar. He would only take money in exchange for work. Dad had only swept the shop out an hour earlier but he gave Haskel the broom. Instead of making a few token sweeps

Haskel conscientiously pushed the broom into every nook and cranny. Then, he asked for a cloth and brush and wiped all the fabric dust from the stock and fitments, ignoring Dad's protests that he had done enough.

He became a frequent visitor to the shop. He pushed a wheelbarrow laden with deliveries, ran errands, cleaned, wrapped parcels and talked with waiting customers so they stayed in the shop while Dad was busy serving another. Although he came from Poland he spoke surprisingly idiomatic English.

Came Passover Dad invited him to spend the first Seder night with us. To participate, said Dad, he would have to sit with us. This sparked off a family furore. Well he is not sitting next to me, we all said in turn. Dad invoked the Old Testament's injunctions to welcome strangers. Mum said it was our duty to make him feel completely at ease. We awaited the first Seder night with mutinous trepidation.

Haskel surprised us all. When he turned up he was clean shaven. He had had a close-trimmed haircut. His black shoes gleamed with polish and he wore a pin-stripe flannel suit with white shirt and matching subdued tie. He carried his belted navy raincoat neatly folded over his arm. He handed Mum a bouquet of cut flowers and he did smell, but of eau de Cologne. The transformation was amazing. As Mary put it, he looked a man any woman would be glad to go out with. He was obviously looking forward to an evening which he had not had for many years. We all felt shame-faced about our earlier resistance to his joining us.

The plentiful flow of the sweet red Carmel wine during that long traditional occasion loosened tongues and Haskel joined in the merry conversations with a will. He revealed that he had been a student at Warsaw University and had planned to be a journalist and writer. But, politically-minded and incautious enough to have written articles that authority regarded as inflammatory he had to flee Poland. It was not difficult for an active Jewish student to fall foul of the police. They had pulled him in for questioning, quite a painful experience, and told him he would be watched carefully. At which point he decided to flee the country. The following Friday night Haskel was back to what Sam called his 'underneath-the-arches-clobber'.

Dad tried hard to persuade him to accompany him to the synagogue. Each time Haskel declined politely. He told Rose 'I don't think I'm one of God's favourites. And, he isn't one of mine. He leaves me alone and I leave him alone. If I have to worship someone, then your parents are my Gods.' He loved to play chess. He beat all of us, winning every game quite easily.

He was poor. What little money he earned he worked hard for and spent carefully. There were no indulgences for Haskel. The only person he trusted with his money was Mum. Whatever he gave her to hold for him she put into a brass pot on the mantelpiece. It was there for him to take out of or put into. Of course, no one else touched it. Apart from the Seder wine that had loosened his tongue he spoke little about himself. When Freda told him that he was intelligent and must have come from a good family Haskel smiled and asked her 'Freda, tell me. What is a good family?'

For three years he came to us until one day, cleaned up and wearing his suit and raincoat and carrying a small case, he strolled into Dad's shop and said that he had come to say goodbye. He had signed on to work passage as a stoker on a ship bound for New York. About six months later Mum received a small parcel from Boston, Massachusetts. It was from Haskel and contained a large intricate silver brooch. He said that he was writing a column for a newspaper and had a flat of his own and was earning well. He wrote that Mum and Dad, especially, but all of us, would always be in his heart as long as he lived. Mum treasured both brooch and letter until the day she died.

Probably my closest friend in the mid-1930s onwards was

Issy Greenstein. Having roped Max, Berl Cohen, a rotund easy-going pupil of Cowper Street school who sang baritone in amateur opera, Norman Myers, a sunny character and zealous cyclist, and myself into *Habonim*, he then talked us into participating in another of his passions. Every Sunday morning Issy and three of us would trek down to the River Lee by Springfield Park and row in a gig four. When we really moved it was exhilarating.

Issy lived in a noisy overcrowded terraced house in Greenwood Road, Dalston, with his father, stepmother, three brothers and two sisters. Privacy there was a dream. Issy had two ambitions; to get to Palestine and play a leading role in the creation of a Jewish State, and to get away from his claustrophobic home.

He was fortunate to have a brain and the will to take him to wherever he wanted to reach. He was popular, easy-going and had the driest sense of humour. In his year he was the youngest pupil at The Grocers to take Matriculation. He passed with distinctions. He passed his Higher Schools examinations with ease. He went onto Birkbeck College, London University, and collected his MA. He never seemed to work harder or longer than others. He spent as much time as we did over Hackney Downs playing football and cricket, but he was able to read a text book just once and extract all the necessary meat out of its contents.

He sang in the choir at Stoke Newington synagogue and, when by himself and even in company, he tended to hum liturgical tunes to himself. This always irritated Max who said that if Issy wanted to walk along looking and sounding daft he, Max, would walk ahead of him. Came the war, he went into the army and made sergeant. He was never posted overseas and he was almost certainly the only British soldier in wartime who mastered the speaking and writing of Hebrew. After an early demobilisation he passed the Civil Service Executive and Administrative exams and went into a branch of the Inland Revenue engaged in plugging loopholes against the tax evaders.

He married Pearly, an ex-ATS corporal, whose home was in Highgate. She was also a member of *Habonim*. He and Pearly were complete opposites. Issy was slim, quiet and thoughtful. She was a large girl, extrovert and impetuous. After the wedding Issy went to live with Pearly in her parents' multi-roomed house and there he found the privacy and quiet that he longed for. They had a son and daughter and I saw very little of Issy. Outside of his work for the Inland Revenue his Zionist activities increased.

In 1948 the British left Palestine and the United Nations partitioned the land into Jewish and Arab territories. Ben Gurion announced the birth of the State of Israel. Seven neighbouring Arab countries marched in determined to wipe out the fledgling Jewish State. The Jews confounded the world by not only surviving but by going on the offensive and finishing up with more land than they had been allocated. Issy was among scores of diaspora Jews with skills and knowledge who flew to Israel to set up the necessary structure of a new democratic country. Issy plunged into the task of helping to set up Israel's local government and civil service along the British lines. For him, it was a dream come true. His family joined him. They set up home in a sunny apartment in Jerusalem. Pearly's mother died of cancer. Her father sold his house in Highgate and went out to live with them. Issy had, by then, changed his name from Greenstein to Gal-Edd.

Issy's abilities and dedication quickly pushed him up the ladder. He became a special adviser to the government on tax and financial matters and ceaselessly travelled with select missions. Israel's priority after the war was to establish a wide industrial base and a strong defence force equipped with the most modern equipment. Every three weeks or so my wife and I would receive a phone call from him, 'Hi. I'm at Heathrow. Can you put me up for a night or two?'

We always obliged. On occasions he would have one or two members of his delegation with him, many of them erstwhile South Africans, Canadians, Americans, a New Zealander and every conceivable European nationality. Now, they were all Israelis. Diaspora communities, especially the American, were providing the money needed to buy plant and machinery for new factories and arms, mainly from Czechoslovakia, and assisting surviving Jews with skills and know-how required by Israel to get there. Those dedicated and tough young men slept cheerfully on a camp bed, on the floor, and provided good company until a car or taxi came to whisk them off to Heathrow airport.

Issy was soon representing Israel at GATT talks in Washington, Geneva, New York and Paris. When he visited America he spoke at fund-raising rallies and banquets and was given royal treatment by leading American Jewry. He was now a very important person and receiving the appropriate treatment. He changed little in himself and was ironically amused at his change of circumstance. A camp bed in the lounge of a Cricklewood semi-detached was replaced by top hotels and chauffeured limousines. Yet, when possible, he still liked to see us, kick off his shoes, sip whisky and dry ginger ale and relax. He had developed gourmet tastes and he often took us out to excellent restaurants, remarking wryly that it was on the house. Strangely, we were much wider apart and yet closer than ever.

He was seldom at home in Jerusalem and his nomadic high-flying life took its toll. He divorced Pearly and married Mirit, a pretty El-Al air hostess. When they came to London they always contrived to take us out. Once, he came alone to London for ten days, an unusually long stay. His job, he said, was to tell Lloyds that henceforth profits earned by Lloyds in Israel would be taxed by the Israeli and not the British Inland Revenue. He finished the negotiations in four days and said it was worth £5 million per annum. 'You've earned your week's wages,' I said.

Another time, with Mirit and my wife, we went down to Lyme Regis for five days' rest. We stayed at the Highcliffe Hotel, once the country home of Sir Joseph Lister, famous for treating surgery with

114

antiseptics and thus reducing drastically the number of post-operative deaths. The weather was English summer at its best. We took long walks around Lyme Bay along the clifftops and Mirit was enchanted with the verdant luxury of the vegetation and the peacefulness of it all. 'Beautiful,' she sighed. 'How wonderful to live here. It's so safe, so pretty, so secure. No wonder it's hard to get English Jews to leave England and come to live in Israel.'

Issy acquired various honours; Director of the Hebrew University, a member of the think tank and many others. Deep down he could never quite get over how far he had soared from that overcrowded house in Dalston. Within a few days of Israel winning the Six Day War he phoned from a London hotel. He sounded fantastically euphoric. He said, 'I'm picking you and Pat up this evening. We're celebrating the victory at the White Tower restaurant. Don't argue. Just be ready.'

He was spot on time. We were driven to that noted restaurant in Percy Street, off Tottenham Court Road, and led up to a large room with a long table laid for about 20. Immediate cocktails sparked off a most memorable night. Pat and I were the only two non-Israelis there. There were men from the embassy, a clutch of VIPs passing through to conferences here and there and, later, Topol, playing the lead in Fiddler on the Roof, *turned up with his wife and some of the cast. The wine flowed. The food was superb. The Greek waiters and managers entered into the spirit of the occasion. There were bursts of impromptu dancing and singing and I recollect Topol, sitting next to me, saying earnestly 'Israel needs families like yours. You, your wife and your two sons. We want you and hundreds like you. We're there to stay and we're going to build a great country.'*

I asked him about Issy, and he said 'A great man. Everyone in Israel knows of him. If he went into politics he would certainly get into the Knesset. But, he likes too much what he is doing.'

During the early 1970s Issy was relaxing in our home with his usual peg of whisky in hand and his shoes kicked off when he suddenly doubled up with pain. He would not let us call for a doctor, saying it was something he had eaten. I drove him back to his West End hotel and we had our usual cheery farewell chat. As he knew, but never told us, he had cancer of the stomach. He knew it was terminal. To the end he worked and presented a brave front. He died within six weeks of our last farewell chat.

When I think of Issy I recall the two *Habonim* summer camps that he persuaded us all to go to. The first was held near Snitterfield, deep in rural Warwickshire, not too far from Stratford-upon-Avon. *Habonim* had rented two large adjoining fields from a farmer, one for boys and the other for girls. Thirty of us went down two weeks before the main camp as pioneers. Issy, Max, Berl, Norman and I were among them.

Our task was to prepare the sites for the main body of campers. In both fields we set up a circle of bell tents, a marquee, rows of showers, latrines and lock-up outhouses for storage. It was scorching hot weather and we worked in shorts and sandals, nothing else. We tanned quickly and became as fit as dancing fleas. The work was hard, especially the digging of trenches for the latrines and drainage. All day long we dripped with sweat and we all developed blisters which broke as we worked. An intense rivalry developed between the two teams as to which would finish their work first. In the boys' field we erected a flagpole. Every morning the Jewish flag was run up to the top of it until sundown. When it went up and was run down we sang the Jewish anthem, *Hatikvah* (The Hope). Berl, the amateur opera singer, could be heard above everyone else. As his mellifluous tones rose and fell Max, always at his grumpiest in the mornings would growl, 'I wonder where he gets his bloody bird seed from.'

After breakfast we washed and sluiced, collected our enamel tin mugs and sat down at long tables to eat the doorstep slices of cottage loaves, cheeses, boiled eggs, tomatoes, apples, milk and cornflakes. We ate as if there was no tomorrow. I have seldom been so content and had such an appetite.

116

From time to time during the day we stopped work and rested on the thick grass, savouring the sun and the stillness of the countryside. Occasionally locals wandered into the fields and wondered what and who we were. We told them we were Jewish. Some found it hard to believe. One said 'You can't be. Jews don't look like you do. You look more like we are . . .' 'Flattery,' retorted the lugubrious Max, 'will get you nowhere.'

Life without the acidity of Max would have been so much duller. After lunch we had a long rest when we could read, stroll, chat up the girls or play cricket. We played with a proper hard ball. On the lush grass it skidded through or reared up even off a good length. We suffered more injuries from cricket than from work. Break over, we worked until 6.30 p.m., then showered and put on the *Habonim* uniform of stockings, clean shorts and shirt. This was *de rigueur*. Standards had to be maintained. Then, in the highest of spirits we would attack the evening meal of baked potatoes, omelettes, viennas, cheese and fruit, followed by those large mugs of hot sweet tea. How we savoured them, sip by sip, as we rested elbows on the table and just talked. I suppose we were Wellesley Aron's dream come to life.

The more romantic would pair off and slide away into the shadows cast by the large trees bordering the fields. Others played chess, draughts, cards or just talked. Some read. The budding musicians played. They included a very good piano accordionist, a flautist and a girl who played the violin with more verve than skill. When their merits were discussed Max observed sourly that of all the bloody fields there were in bloody Warwickshire, she had to play in the same bloody field he was in.

Erecting the stages in the marquee was a job none of us had ever tackled. How to do it best was the cause of so much disputation that at times we were all site managers and no workers. By trial and error we got it up. To test it, ten of us

117

stood on it and jumped up and down. Twice it collapsed and we all suffered bruises and cuts. Everyone watching thought it was very funny. A German boy, Didi, took charge. He spoke good English and said 'Listen. I know what to do. None of you have any idea. So, just do what I tell you and we'll get it up properly.' We agreed, did what he told us, and the stage was as firm as the rock of Gibraltar. We finished the work on schedule and the next day we were joined by some 150 boys and girls. About half were German, Austrian and Czecho-slovakian refugees.

A thick five foot high hedgerow divided the two camps. A five-barred gate in the middle of it gave the only means of entry from one field to another. The gate was open up to the lowering of the flag. When that came down the gate was closed and no boys were permitted to stray into the girls' field and vice versa. At night, four camp officers, in their thirties, walked along the dividing hedge to ensure that camp rules were adhered to. Of course, human ingenuity contrived to defeat both rules and officers.

We slept six to a tent with heads against the canvas and feet towards the centre pole. All our possessions had to be kept tidily inside our sixth of the tent. Issy, Berl, Norman, Max and I were together with a boy named Roddy. Max was the tidiest, a fact he was not at all modest about. Living in such close proximity made us aware of one another's habits and short-comings. When the rest of us were yawning into a deep sleep Norman would want to talk.

'I can't sleep. Are you chaps awake?'

'Yes, you bloody fool. Now, shut up.'

Issy tended to lie on his back, arms folded back under his head, contentedly humming away until the irascible Max would tell him to put a sock in it. Earwigs fell onto blankets. One startled Norman by landing on his face. I said, 'They're dangerous. They penetrate your ear and burrow right into your brain.'

118

'How can they?' from Max. 'He hasn't got one.'

'Idiots,' muttered Norman. I noticed that he surreptitiously covered his exposed ear with the blanket.

'Better close your mouth,' advised Berl. 'If one falls into it, it will walk down your throat and come out the other end. Very painful. It happened to an aunt of mine.'

'Oh, balls,' cursed Norman. He pressed his lips together. Berl and I exchanged grins.

The tent had one opening, a panel which opened from top to bottom all the way down one side and could be secured from the inside by a line of toggles. Berl, by the opening, always wanted to close it. The rest of us insisted upon keeping it open. Berl demanded to change places with someone, any-one. No one took up his offer. During the night when someone wanted to visit the latrine, bodies and legs were trodden on and curses filled the air. Also, when the flap was opened wide to let someone out or in Berl was always disturbed from sleep. He got very fed up with all this and the fifth night he rebelled. After Max had trodden on Berl and told him to watch where he was sleeping, the worm turned. Berl closed the flap and secured all the inside toggles. When Max returned and found the panel closed he was furious.

'Let me in, you silly buggers,' he barked. He shook the tent and pounded the canvas with his fists. 'I'll collapse the bloody thing on top of you.'

In reply, Berl pulled his blanket over his head. Max raged on about stupid buggers playing at silly buggers and how next time he would not go out but do what he had to do over Berl.

'He's kicking at the pegs', cried Roddy. 'Let him in.'

Berl did not move. Issy stretched across the mutinous mound and without saying a word undid the toggles. No one spoke as Max, breathing fire at all and sundry, just flopped down and snuggled under his blankets. We were falling asleep again when Norman said plaintively 'I'm fully awake now. I don't think I can sleep any more. Can you?' A menacing rumble came from Max. 'Kill him, somebody. Just kill him.'

One night a girl's terrified screams aroused both camps. Shriek followed shriek of sheer terror. Boys and officers raced into the girls' camp. Bewildered and frightened, they were milling about in night dress and undress. In one tent, where the flap had been left open, a girl had awakened to find looming over her a large head with bulging eyes and hot breath, so she screamed and screamed and screamed. It had turned out to be an inquisitive bull or heifer which had somehow wandered into the field through a gate that was found to be open. Her screams had scared the beast and when we all rushed into the field flashing torches and shouting the animal hurried back whence it came. The girl was German. Her English was minimal. It took a long time to calm her down.

We soon became a local attraction. Villagers came and mingled with us and this led to a sports day between them and us. The event spread over two days. It was arranged by our camp leader and the local vicar, who looked after several parishes. When he came to visit us during the pioneer days and learned that we were Jewish he became a frequent visitor. He called us People of the Book. Embarrassingly, he knew far more of the Old Testament than we did.

The first event was a soccer match. We won by three goals to one. I was centre forward and scored the first and third. The third was a long range volley on the turn. As I fell over I heard an exuberant female voice yell 'I never did like that boy but I could kiss him for that.'

It was the ebullient Pearly, who later married Issy. We beat them at cricket and at most field events, where our German and Austrian boys excelled. All the games were played in very good spirits and the last day culminated with an enormous bonfire with a barbecue, music and dancing. It started at 8 p.m. and went on well past midnight. Many villagers turned up, whole families, through curiosity as much else, and the fact that we were Jews confounded some of them. We were nothing

120

like they had expected Jews to be. It made some of us wonder whether the poisonous caricatures of Jews promulgated by Goebbels and Julius Streicher had seeded in Warwickshire.

One of the three Christian clergy who came to enjoy the evening explained.

> Some of them have never met a Jew. To them a Jew is a Shylock, or a Fagin, always an unsavoury character. You could blame English literature for that. Jews have always been baddies. Pick up a book by Edgar Wallace, John Buchan and Dorothy L. Sayers and try to find one Jewish character on the side of the angels. Here, they see happy sunburnt boys and girls. Half of you are fair-haired and blue-eyed and there's not a beard or black gaberdine cloak to be seen anywhere. You beat them at all the games and sports and Jews just don't play them. What they see here conflicts with what they have always believed . . . and that's a very good thing.

At the end of the party our musicians gathered to play for a final sing-song. The accordionist gave a solo, then the flautist and then the girl violinist. Seeing her, Max groaned 'Our guests may not be anti-semitic now, but they will be after she plays to them.' The sing-song ended. There was hand-shaking and expressions of goodwill all round. The log fire was reduced to glowing embers and thoroughly doused with water and then it was all over. As we trudged back to our tent Berl said, 'I'm knackered. I don't want my sleep disturbed at all. So go to the latrines now because if one of you goes out I'll close the flap and he'll never get in again.'

'You do that,' threatened Max, 'and I'll find a sharp stick and poke it under the canvas and keep jabbing you. I know where to find you.'

Issy laughed, 'You're like Blackpool rock, Max. Slice you anywhere and you're still the same cantankerous sod.'

Late in 1943 my ship berthed in Alexandria and I went ashore with my shipmate, a Lancastrian double for George Formby named Bill Kenneford. He came from Oswaldtwistle. In a bar my eye caught a sun-blackened army sergeant dressed in an unusually casual fashion. He wore suede shoes and had a silk scarf tucked into an open-necked shirt. It was Didi, the German boy who had supervised the erection of the marquee stage at Snitterfield. He said he was on a short leave after a spell in the desert with Popski's private army. I thought it was a joke. Later, of course, I learned that it was a free-booting long-range desert group which operated behind the German lines creating havoc where they could. It was led by an audacious Pole named Popski. Didi's role, wearing an Afrika Korps uniform and speaking fluent German, was to fool German sentries into not sensing danger until it was too late. He said that the two weeks at the Snitterfield camp had been the happiest time of his life. If he survived the war he would go to Palestine. But, if I ever passed Snitterfield, give it his love. That was his request to me as we parted.

In the summer of 1972 I was driving back from Birmingham to London. I was in no hurry. I deliberately detoured and passing through idyllic countryside I eventually reached Snitterfield. It seemed to be a well manicured up-market dormitory town. I walked about and asked a few elderly people if they remembered the camp. None did. I headed out into the countryside and a strange gust of déjà vu swept over me. It was so strong that I stopped the car by a farm. Hedgerows had been destroyed to placate the Gods of intensive farming but there were two familiar adjacent fields. Tall trees lined their perimeters. As I stared, I said out aloud, 'Yes, This is it. We were here.'

I leaned against the car and smoked a small cigar and remembered. Issy, dead of cancer. Max, who became a sergeant-pilot and was posted to a Beaufighter squadron in East Anglia, was downed in a dogfight over the North Sea. He was posted missing. His body was never found. Roddy died in a Japanese prisoner of war camp. Norman who, after being demobilised from the RAF, developed a thriving children's entertainment business specialising in parties for top people's progeny.

122

The two pretty blonde sisters from Brno who all the boys tried to date without success. They were only intent on getting to Palestine. Did they make it? Berl? He went into the army and we completely lost touch. And Didi? Did he survive the war and, if he went to Palestine, did he survive fighting for Israel in its wars, as he certainly would have done? Before I drove off I stared at the two fields and said, 'Didi sends you his love.'

Chapter Ten

Every classroom carried a large map of the world. British possessions were coloured in red. At least one quarter of all the land denoted the extent of the British Empire. It was a dishonest British-born Jew who said that he did not feel pride in the achievements of his countrymen and the whole country celebrated Empire Day one way or another. At the same time, across the North Sea, the Nazis were feverishly preparing for invasions that would soon colour massive chunks of Europe in black.

But, we had the school battalion. We looked forward to it as a fun day. From a military training point of view it was a joke. Once during each term the entire school including all masters assembled in the spacious front playground. The 800-odd boys were divided into four companies, A, B, C and D. Each boy was given a wooden rifle and ex-regimental sergeant major Marley came into his own, putting us through the basics of drill. How he revelled in those battalion days when everyone, including masters, obeyed his bellowed commands.

His boots gleamed like black plastic. His long thin moustache was waxed to needle point sharpness at both its ends. His chest, carrying his row of medals, vied with his stomach to see which could protrude furthest forward. He carried a silver knobbed walking stick tightly tucked under his left arm and as he marched to and fro, his stiffened right arm swung in a complete semi-circle from in front to behind and back again.

He had us forming fours, sloping arms, ordering arms, presenting arms, grounding arms, turning left, turning right, coming to attention and standing at ease. But boys did tend to muck about and tangles did occur. On one terrible occasion my D company found itself marching down the slope in the direction of the railway line while the other three companies headed in the opposite direction. I saw Marley, puce with anger and exertion, hurtling towards us. He roared 'And where does bloody D company think it is going?'

'To catch the 2.30 from Hackney Downs station to Lower Edmonton,' some bright spark shouted back.

Not only did we halt but we staggered about laughing. Our officers and NCOs, masters and sixth formers, tried to quell us but even they could not keep straight faces. Marley had the last word however. Only on Battalion Day did he have authority to issue punishment on his own account. He looked grimly triumphant as he strode along the ragged lines of the now quiet D company and boomed.

'You will all write out five hundred times the following message: "Mucking about on Battalion Day is a serious breach of discipline. I will never do it again".'

That sobered us up very quickly. The high spot came when in columns of four we marched out of the school main gates behind our band as it brassed out stirring military marches. We marched around Hackney Downs and back into Amhurst Road, left along its length, under the iron railway bridge, left into Bodney Road and left again into Downs Park Road and back into the school. There we were dismissed and told to go home. Somehow, I doubt whether we would have impressed the boys from Soest.

Our battalion aroused hostile comment from pacifists who declared they wanted to prevent the boys from developing a jingoistic military mind. We felt they had a damned cheek trying to spoil a good day's outing. The only harm Battalion Day did was to Marley's blood pressure. He took it very much to heart that he could never get our lines ramrod straight. Battalion was stopped in 1965.

September, High Holydays apart, was the watershed month of every year. Summer and the last games of county cricket were both fading away fast. The evenings carried the first autumnal nip in the air and there were the first morning mists. There were falling leaves being whipped along by rising winds, hot porridge for breakfast and warmer clothing. In the greengrocer's the soft luscious cherries, strawberries and gooseberries had given way to plums, pears, nuts and the scrunchy cox pippin apple. Worst of all it rained more, which interfered with our playing of flickers on the wider pavements.

Flickers was another exciting schoolboy game that halted when wartime austerity stopped cigarette firms from inserting stiffening cards into their packets. There were Players, Kensitas, Passing Clouds, Wills, de Reszke and so many varieties of makes and each brand inserted their distinctive cards into each packet. After the war those cigarette cards became collectors' items and increased very much in value. No ephemera exhibition would be complete without them. The glossy cards were so attractive, showing a coloured illustration of a flower, a ship, a film star, an animal, a bird, a cricketer, anything and everything. The reverse side of the cards gave a potted description of the item on the front of it. Each card was numbered. The number of cards required to make up a set ranged from 30 up to 50. The trick was to make complete sets which could be sold for useful pocket money. School breaks would see noisy groups holding frenetic exchange and marts.

'I need British regiments numbers four, 26 and 32 to complete my set.'

'I've got Hollywood stars. And I've got the one you want. Carole Lombard. I want a penny for it.'

'I haven't got money. I'll give you swaps.'

'Don't want swaps. I want a penny.'

'Halfpenny and six swaps?'

Money was money. 'Done.'

No Persian market saw keener haggling. Boys sold their souls to complete sets. Grown-ups everywhere were badgered by boys to buy the brands containing their sets, the ones they were accumulating. I pestered Mick and Sam when they started to smoke. The most popular way to get cards was by playing flickers. Between two and six boys would line up at the kerb of a wide pavement – Amhurst Road was ideal – the first boy would flick his card up against the low brick wall of the front garden on the other side of the pavement and each boy, in turn, would flick a card. The first boy who landed a card on top of one of those on the pavement would scoop the pool. It grew quite nerve-wracking when a haul of 50-plus cards were there for the taking. The joy of the winner was unrestrained and then it was his turn to flick the first card for the next round. Passers-by were always kind enough to step into the roadway. Dogs would be frightened away by a chorus of shouts.

September meant conkers. As the prickly green casings dropped, split open and shed their glossy brown horse chestnuts boys would seek out their favourite trees with bags containing a variety of missiles. Up to a dozen boys would stand under the same spreading leafy trees throwing their half bricks, stones and short thick chunks of wood upwards to knock down the nuts. Many a boy was dented by the falling debris and arguments and fights did break out. It all added to the excitement.

The ensuing weeks saw groups of boys surrounding two conker protagonists, each trying to disintegrate his opponent's conker with blows from his own. The receiver held out at arm's length a piece of string at the bottom of which dangled his conker. His opponent swung his conker downwards to try and hit the other one. Sometimes the swung conker completely missed its target and completed the loop by painfully striking the back of the hand that wielded it. Boys strove to harden their conkers by many ingenious means; soaking them in vinegar, slow boiling them and even spreading a patina of colourless glue over them.

The object of the game was to possess the highest scoring conker. If you destroyed another's conker, yours became a oner. If you won against a conker that was, say, a fiver, then your oner would become a sixer. Twentyers were prized. Thirtyers were a rarity and the boy whose battle-scarred veteran reached the dizzy heights of being a fiftyer took it out of the fight and mounted it on a small wooden plinth.

Cob nuts generated a game called knockout. A circle was chalked on a pavement or floor and up to six boys would each place an agreed number of nuts in the circle. Standing or crouching by a mark some six feet from the circle, the participants would take it in turns to throw or roll other cobs at those encircled. Those knocked out of the circle were kept by the thrower.

During the school holidays it was football and cricket that superseded every other activity. Every day saw every field over Hackney Downs filled with arguing, running, shouting, swearing boys. For Jewish boys Saturday afternoons were hazardous. After synagogue and a rushed lunch, not daring to take off my good suit and alert Dad, I would sneak to the Downs and participate in one of the many games being played. I would pair off with another waiting boy, take off my jacket and add it to the small pile that formed one of the goalposts and then plunge into the game. From time to time a Jewish boy would cry out 'I'll be back' and run off to conceal himself until his father or someone who would tell his father about his son's desecration of the Sabbath would be out of sight. Thus, a team of 11 could be reduced to ten and even to nine. Unwary boys hearing their fathers call angrily from the touchline would shout 'Get someone to take my place. I won't be back.' Back home the errant boys would receive chastisement, which became less physical and more verbal the older they became.

I always felt safe because I knew that Dad spent his Sabbath afternoons ensconced in the dining room, studying the Talmud and dozing. However, one Saturday afternoon I was happily playing football when I was suddenly unnerved by the sight of Dad and Mr Cohen strolling along the path in our direction. Shouting 'It's my Dad. I'm off. I'll be back . . .' I scooted for the perimeter and hid lurking behind a tree. To my utter dismay I saw Dad and Mr Cohen sit down on a bench and watch the game. I could not go away because my jacket helped to form a goalpost. For half an hour I fretted behind that tree, enduring acid comments from passing women.

'That boy's up to no good, I'll wager . . .'

'He's been there a long time. What's he up to?'

'Disgusting, some of 'em. Doesn't he know there's a convenience by the centre?'

The game ended. Dad and Mr Cohen remained on that bench, enjoying the sunshine and talking. I agonised. My jacket. But, a friend who played and saw my predicament brought it over to me. I made a circuitous detour back to the house. When Dad arrived home he said to me, 'It's shameful. I saw Rappaport and Miller's boys playing football over the Downs. On *Shemini Atzeret*, too. I hope you have more respect.'

'Of course, Dad.'

'Well don't let me catch you.'

'You won't, Dad' I promised, really meaning it.

Those halcyon days had hazards. As football and cricket games intermingled, cricket balls would hurtle across football games, narrowly missing and occasionally hitting a boy. Dogs were always a nuisance. Football excited them and they often joined in, chasing the balls and barking with the fun of it. Some regarded the clothing goalposts as trees and tended to cock their legs against them. It was the duty of goalkeepers to prevent this happening. When they dozily failed to do so they would be roundly berated by boys whose clothes had been baptised.

The players could make a strange mix. Jews, communists and blackshirts, fully aware of what one another were, played amicably enough. That same evening they could be viciously fighting one another. Sport was sport. Politics was politics. That was England.

The immigrant generation never went near a pub and during the 1930s very few of their sons and daughters went into them. It was not a Jewish scene. But every Jewish person regarded himself and herself as an expert on food. Highlights of weddings and barmitzvahs were not the ceremonies or even the bands and the dancing but the quality of the food and drink that was served.

The merits of caterers like Monnickedam, Schaverien and others were discussed with the same passion that was aroused between the supporters of the Tottenham and Arsenal football clubs when they argued the merits of their teams. But the food I enjoyed the most was made by Goide's. They had a shop-cum-eaterie close by the Whitechapel Art Gallery and served up light tasty luncheons. Their cakes were mouth-watering, especially their varieties of almond and cheese cakes. The father was a tall dignified bespectacled man with a grave demeanour. His two sons were clones. It was strange to see those three tall figures with identical yarmulkas together. But it was Jean who dominated that comfortable place, so much so that people would say 'I'll met you at Jean's for lunch.'

She had thickly painted lips, rouged cheeks and dyed blonde hair that framed her head like a tea cosy with its front cut away. She was a dynamo in a wraparound white coat, a perfect example of perpetual motion allied to a non-stop flow of chatter. She took orders, served behind the counter, manned the till, disappeared in and out of the kitchen, rushed out to tell impatient customers to wait a bit and was into everything that happened. She ran the place, even when the Goides were there. She would tell them 'Just you leave it to me. You go away' and they would smile and do as she said. Even the large black cat obeyed Jean. When she pointed a finger at it and ordered 'You. Disappear. You know you shouldn't be here lunchtime' the cat would look hurt and stroll back into the kitchen and not be seen again until later that afternoon.

We agreed that she was the best saleswoman ever. She was popular even with the customers she scolded and chided and had Goide's sacked her we would all have risen up in protest. But, she could handle them. If a Goide ventured a suggestion Jean would raise her hands palms outwards to them and say 'Just leave it to me.' The Goide in question would sigh and go away. If she took a liking to a customer he would get service par excellence and a three-egg omelette for the same price as a two-egger. If he wanted a second coffee she would not charge him for it.

Goide's went through the war and into the 1950s with Jean always in charge. She greeted every returned demobbed customer with a smacking kiss on the cheek and a free meal. The Goides shrugged and blind-eyed the loss in takings. Jean's value was indeed a sum beyond rubies. It was her undeniable cheeky irresistible salesmanship that we loved to witness. Along the counter upon which stood the till was a delectable array of Goide's produces: almond and cheese cakes, doughnuts as light as feathers, chocolate sponge and sachertortes *and everything to tempt the sweet tooth. When a customer proffered a high denomination note to pay for his lunch Jean would glide into action. She would hold the note and, waving her hand at the confection filling the counter top would say 'Now, which of these would you like to take home to your lovely family. You know your family will kiss you for your thoughtfulness. How about these. You want half a dozen? No? Then you probably want these . . . there I'll put them in a bag for you.' And she did. Still clutching the note she would start putting six of a fresh delight into a bag saying 'These are out of this world . . .' The bemused customer's protests grew feebler and feebler and he would be reduced to pleading 'Jean, for God's sake give me what you want and my change, what's left of it, and let me get out of here.'*

'What a lovely man,' Jean would say loudly as she handed over the change and the purchases. 'See how he thinks of his family. The world would be a better place if there were more like him.' Her parting shot that the customer would return for more often proved right. In a strange alchemic way Jean's customers became her friends. None could deny her. On the other hand she looked after them and gave ungrudging motherly service. It was said that once she had been on the stage. When asked, she never affirmed or denied it but would reply mysteriously 'Ah. You'd never believe the things I got up to when I was young.'

In the late 1950s the Goides closed down their Whitechapel restaurant. They still catered and opened a small retail corner shop in Commercial Street to sell what they baked. Jean ran this shop. She had two assistants, very old ladies who could barely stand upright and actually tottered when they walked. It was a bizarre place but the breads and rolls and cakes still smelled and tasted good. They were always making excellent cafetiered coffee for themselves. One day I went in to buy an almond cake and Jean said suddenly, 'I've always liked you. Would you like some coffee?' I drank it and proffered payment. Jean refused to take it and said, 'You can always have a coffee if you're passing by. By the way, where do you lunch?'

'Oh, anywhere I can snatch a sandwich and coffee.'

'Not good enough,' snapped Jean. 'You bring in some smoked salmon and we'll make up delicious salmon rolls for you. And what with our cakes you'll have a nice lunch.'

Many times over the next few years I slid into one of the many delicatessen shops in Hessel Street and bought a quarter of a pound of smoked salmon and crispy new green cucumbers and took them to Jean. She would make up the sandwiches or beigels and sit me at a small table and leave me alone to eat and read. Now and again a passer-by seeing me eating would call in for a snack.

'We're not a restaurant, we just sell what we show,' Jean would say.

'What about him?' pointing to me.

'He's an old friend.'

'I see.' The disappointed man would waver and then turn to go. At which point Jean's predatory instincts rose to the fore.

'Here . . .' She would give that wide smile. 'I'm sorry. But while you're here have one of these cheesecakes. They're still warm. They're delicious. Go on. It's on the house. You don't have to pay for it.' The man would eat it and nod his head appreciatively. The hook swallowed, Jean started to reel in.

'I'll tell you what,' again that wide smile, 'as you're such a nice man I can't refuse you a lunch. Sit down there and I'll make you up a nice cheese platzel or an egg and tomato roll and make you some coffee. Then, of course, you must, simply must have a slice of our wonderful almond cake.'

When the man departed he would have added considerably to the shop's takings with a filled carrier bag. One day Jean broke the sad news. The Goides had sold the shop. I asked her what she would do.

'Do?' She looked genuinely surprised. 'What do you mean? I'll get another job, of course. I'm only 71 and any boss would be glad to have a worker like me.'

She was serious. The following week I had lunch in the shop in the usual way. Jean was her busy conscientious self and we exchanged our usual banter. A few days later it was all over. The shop was closed. The heavy padlocks on the doors spelled out finality itself. I looked through the window. The inside of the shop was completely bare. The counters, tables, chairs and shelves had all gone. It was desolation itself. Jean's singular verve and talents deserved a much better reward than they received.

Chapter Eleven

The ideals of *Habonim* were getting under our skins. When Jews felt secure, as we did in England, striving for a National Home tended to take a very far back seat. Yet the determined visionaries of Zionists like Issy did disturb our complacency. We began to become very loyal to the *Habonim* movement and as a result Issy, Max, Berl, Norman and I again went to the *Habonim* summer camp the year following Snitterfield. We did not go on pioneer. We shared a tent with an Austrian boy who we called Putzi. Putzi planned to become a doctor and he was obsessed with mastering the English language well enough to enable him to pass the required examinations. He went into deep depressive moods. He felt guilty at being safe in England while his parents and two sisters were in danger in Graz. He was slim, dark-haired, quiet and very introverted. He made a likeable companion.

The stay was memorable for a legendary outing that became hilariously known as 'the long walk'. I suggested it and never lived the fact down. Putzi preferred to go down to the Christchurch waterfront and see the very large geese and swans so we five set out straight after lunch into the sunny idyllic countryside. We frolicked merrily through bluebell-covered dales and across gentle hills, over stiles and across fields that could have been private. We meandered through woodland and sometimes followed ramblers' paths. We rested a few times and as we were sprawling contentedly in a field of bluebells and daisies Norman said, 'Hey, you chaps. Do you realise that it's six o'clock. I'm starving. We'd better make our way back for supper.' Simultaneously we all realised that we were lost. We had no idea where we were, nor in which direction lay the camp. We had no maps. Galvanised by the thought of missing the evening meal we started walking, but when we came to a signpost that said Somewhere we had no idea where Somewhere was in relation to the camp.

Max decided to take charge. He said, 'Sometimes I wonder where you lot keep your brains. Follow me.'

He set off at such a brisk pace and so decisively that we were convinced that he knew where he was going. So we followed him. After about 20 minutes he perceptibly slowed and Issy sing-songed 'I fear the worst'.

Hunger and fatigue tarnished Norman's natural ebullience. He cried out, 'The bloody fool has gone wrong. He's been leading us in the wrong direction. You can tell by the sun.'

Max, in accordance with his nature, eschewed defence and apology and rounded on Norman, 'Listen to bloody Christopher Columbus . . .'

'We should be going east,' broke in Norman, 'and you've been leading westwards.'

'You'll go west in a moment if you don't shut up,' growled Max. 'If you thought I was wrong why did you follow me?'

'Hey!' Issy shouted as he stood up. 'Quarrelling will get us nowhere. Let's sit down and think it out.'

'That,' said Max, 'discounts Norman. He can't think because he hasn't got a brain.'

Norman ignored him and said, 'Has anyone got any chocolate. I'm ravenous.'

'Christ,' said Max, continuing to divert attention away from his mistake, 'that's all he thinks of, his guts.'

Meanwhile, Berl, who had slumped to the ground and rested with his back against a tree, uttered a plea, 'I can't face walking in the wrong direction again. Let's ask someone.'

'Oh, go away and sing an aria,' snapped Max. 'We haven't seen anyone for years. We don't know the name of the farm we're camped on. We don't know the name of the farmer. We don't know whether we're in Hampshire or Dorset. And,' glaring at me, 'as for the moron who thought up the idea . . .'

'You didn't have to come along,' I said.

'And leave you scruffy lot loose in this green and pleasant land?' scoffed Max. 'It wouldn't have been fair to the natives.'

'We're lost,' moaned the pathetic Berl. 'We really are lost . . .'

'Bloody genius.' Max clapped his hands in mock applause. 'However did you work that one out?'

'All right. All right.' Issy raised his arms for peace and said authoritatively. 'Let's look at the facts. When we left the camp did we walk straight across the field opposite the gate? Did we turn left or did we turn right? But before we get onto that, Max, when you set out so confidently, did you have any idea where you were going?'

'Certainly,' said Max. 'I was going to have a leak. I'm shy. So, when you all followed, I just kept going . . .' We all sighed. Max walked away and perched sulkily on the top bar of a nearby gate. The sun was lowering down to the horizon at gathering speed. Light was beginning to fade and we felt more than a little anxious. Being lost was bad enough but to think of our camp mates tucking into food and drink hit us hardest of all. My ears burned as I heard Max talking generally, 'Bloody stupid twit, suggesting a walk. Why didn't he just play cricket like he always does?'

In desperation Berl asked, 'Has anyone got a compass?'

'Sure,' called Max. 'And I've got a ship's log and a chronometer and a sextant and a book of tables. I always carry them with me when I go on a walk.'

'A compass will show us where we're going,' protested Berl.

'Sure,' replied Max. 'Trouble is we don't know where we are going so what use is a compass?'

Issy, who had been sitting quietly, suddenly took charge. He said, 'When we left the camp we crossed the road and plunged straight across that field into some woods. We were heading away from the sea, therefore we were going north. After that we turned eastwards and paralleled the coast, more or less. Then, we went through a water meadow, going north again, and then we took a dirt track that took us north-westerly . . .' He went on like this listing estimated distances travelled in which directions and concluded, 'We've been away for five and a half hours. Say we've travelled about seven to eight miles, we must be within five miles of the camp.'

'Five miles,' echoed Berl piteously. 'Oh, God.' He lay back on the grass and closed his eyes. Norman confessed that he had never felt so faint. I decided that I would play cricket every afternoon until the camp ended.

Issy continued his train of thought. 'We must head south. This will take us in the general direction of the camp. We'll just keep going and ask everyone we meet until we hit lucky. So, on your feet, southwards it is . . .'

'Which way is south?' worried Norman.

'The opposite direction to bloody north, you idiot.'

Berl chipped in. 'What happens if we keep going and come to the sea? What do we do then?'

'That's easy. As far as you are concerned,' advised Max, 'just keep going until you hit France.'

In single file we followed a chirpy humming Issy, as forlorn a group as you could ever meet. After a 30-minute trudge with heads down in the deepening dark Issy stopped. He raised a warning arm and hissed, 'Shush. A cyclist is coming towards us.'

It was a farm labourer, pedalling wearily homeward on his old bone-shaker after a hard day's work. He was at peace with the world until we stepped from the shadows of that very minor road and Issy sang out, 'Stop, please. Can you help us?'

Whoever accused farm labourers of being slow on the uptake maligned them. That cyclist, as quick as a flash, realised that his life was in danger. He had a choice of options. He could jump off his bike and run into the woods to safety or he could do what he did. Somehow, he increased speed as he rode at us. As we backed away he swerved violently and was through us. We watched him wobble precariously for several yards hoping that he would fall off but momentum reasserted balance. With an Olympian spurt of energy he sped fast into the deep gloom.

'Miserable sod,' Max yelled hopelessly after him. 'I hope you get two punctures.'

'Look at us,' sighed Issy. 'Five evil-looking footpads. Wouldn't you be scared in his shoes?'

Unexpectedly, Berl exploded with uncontrollable mirth. He collapsed and rolled about on the road. 'He's gone mad,' said Max. 'I knew it would happen. Let's turn him loose in the forest.'

Berl recovered, gulping air, and he gasped, 'Just think of the tale he'll tell in his local tonight, how five evil-looking villains leaped out at him and how he just managed to escape with his life . . .'

As tired, hungry and as fed up as we were, we all had to laugh. The word 'local' set Norman off again and he moaned that the canteen would now be shut, the food stores padlocked, and he wondered if the camp would send out search parties.

'For you?' exclaimed Max. 'They'll be glad to get rid of you. That would at least give the girls a rest.'

We trudged on and on and on. Talk became desultory. Norman kept wondering how many miles we had walked.

'Too bloody many,' exploded Max.

'I only asked a civil question.'

'Civil, but daft. What matters is how many more we have to walk.'

138

'It's a lovely night,' observed Issy. 'We could sleep out under the stars.'

'I do,' muttered Berl. 'Every bloody night with you selfish sods leaving that flap open.' We were all a bit concerned about Berl. He staggered along gallantly but we could see that he was on the verge of collapse. He shrugged away supportive hands. Issy kept humming to himself. Norman wondered if there were mushrooms to be found. Berl expressed a longing to sit down. I pointed out that if he did so he would find it hard to get up. Berl said that it was safe rural England, not the jungle or the Sahara. Max suggested that when he sat down he should keep a diary of his last moments for posterity. Then, when his skeleton was found the diary would make him as famous as Scott of the Antarctic. Passing through thick undergrowth we all suffered a mass of scratches and stings on our stockingless legs. It was a beautiful night with a very bright moon and a cloudless star-filled sky.

We knew that we were hopelessly lost. Berl was flagging so badly we seriously discussed finding a barn or haystack or any shelter to lie up in for the night. Norman went on about his stomach and finding a pub. We were walking along a narrow winding footway beside a six-line wire fence when we were halted by a shouted hostile command.

'You lot, there. Halt, or I'll open fire.'

A powerful torch was shone into our faces and two farmers, father and son, each carrying a shotgun, emerged from a nearby gate. The guns were at the ready and they were definitely not pleased to see us. The father said angrily, 'We've been watching you. What the hell are you doing here this time of night?'

We said that we were just following a footpath for walkers. The farmer spat, 'Footpath for walkers, my arse. It's our land and we're damned sick of bloody trespassers like you so you'd better get off it, and quickly!

Max bristled and showed every sign of engaging in an

argument. Issy hastily stepped in front of him and explained that we were lost and were looking for our camp. Did the farmer, perchance, know where it was?. The farmer knew of no damned camp. The son then spoke for the first time.

'There is one. They were talking about it in the pub last night. Lots of foreigners, boys and girls.'

'This lot speak good English for foreigners,' scowled the father. He stared at us. 'Well? Are you foreigners?'

'Of course,' said Max caustically, 'we're from London.'

The farmer nodded his head. 'That's foreign enough for me.'

Issy was talking to the son and elicited that the camp was on a farm next to the farm of a friend of his. The son referred to a hamlet that we knew was close by the camp. Issy asked how far away was it.

'Not more than two miles,' said the farmer's son.

I heard Berl gasp. 'Two more miles. I can't make it. I just can't.'

He did, just, helped by our taking it in turns to link arms with him and literally dragging him along. It was at midnight, ten hours after we had set out, that we reached the camp. We sneaked across to the food storehouse. It was closed and firmly padlocked. One of the duty officers came up to us and wondered what the hell we were doing. We told him about the walk. He laughed fit to bust, Norman pleaded that he couldn't go to bed without some food. But, that was no go. No food. Issy told Norman to imagine it was *Yom Kippur*. We awakened Putzi when we stumbled into the tent. He was pleased to see us and started to tell us about the most interesting large birds he had seen that day.

'Putzi,' snarled Max, 'if you bloody well want to live long enough to speak English properly, bloody well shut up about those bloody birds.'

'All right,' agreed Putzi equably, 'but can you tell me the significance in the English language of the word "bloody". Why is it used so often?'

We fell into our sleeping bags without even changing into our pyjamas. No one disturbed Berl that night. The next day all the other campers pulled our legs mercilessly but never had a breakfast or lashings of hot sweet tea tasted so good. It did wonders for our dehydration. That afternoon it was back to cricket.

Those two camps were highlights. It made its members aware of their roots and motivated many Jewish boys and girls into going to Palestine to work in kibbutzim and on the land. Thus *Habonim* made a fractional but valuable contribution to the creation of the Jewish State.

Chapter Twelve

Mum was always too fatigued and busy to lift her nose from the grindstone and be aware of, let alone have any interest in, the racist politics of fascism swirling around her. When she was not mending and repairing and shopping she was busy cooking, frying, baking, boiling, pickling and preserving. Her efforts filled the large cold larder. It was always a gastronomic Aladdin's cave. The ever lean and ravenous Aubrey liked to sneak inside and filch the goodies. Mary knew this. She would ambush him and tweak his ear and haul him out of it, scolding 'Howie, you don't want to keep your mother at the stove all the time. She's prepared food for four days for everyone. So, hop it.'

Mum's only real pleasure apart from her weekly outing to the cinema with her friends were the flower beds in our back garden. Her pride and joy was the rectangular flower bed just outside the kitchen window filled with six rows of her favourite geraniums in red, white and pink. In summer she sat by the opened window and gazed out at them, savouring their colour and musky smell.

Adjacent to the flower bed was a paved area just twice its size on which the four of us played furious two-a-side games of football. Two goals had been chalked out on the opposing walls. During the games the ball and a shoulder-charged body would crash onto that flower bed. Geraniums would be broken. We would stick the snapped stems back into the earth, but they soon wilted. This brought us under the stern disapproval of George the gardener. He would collect the casualties and reprimand us severely. We did apologise and we did feel guilty, but our passion for football kept us playing.

George was a Devonian and spoke with a pleasing West Country burr. He was a large, slow man, deliberate in movement, his muscles softening into fat. He had a round weathered face with bushy side whiskers and strands of white hair blowing backwards over a sunburnt dome. His very substantial belly strained forward so tightly against a two-inch wide belt that Mary joked that if he undid it he would explode. He wore thick black serge trousers which dropped onto an enormous pair of black army boots. These were so highly polished, they reflected sunlight like a mirror. He had very alert light-blue eyes and he was a most equable man, except when he saw a new crop of damaged geraniums. He spoke slowly, masticating his thoughts before putting them into words. He was no fool, an interesting man to talk to and he was never so angry as when he was defending Mum against the depradations of her sons against her flower beds. When he arrived in the morning for his day's work in our garden, he came once a week, he went to the shed for the garden tools and the same comedy routine was played out. Mum would take him in a tray of tea and her home-made strudels and butter biscuits. The huge genial George would raise his hands and protest 'Thankee, missus, but I had a large breakfast not so long ago.'

'So? A big man like you needs plenty of food.'

'Thankee, but I'm not hungry . . .'

'If you don't eat properly, you can't work well.'

'Dear, oh dear.' George would shake his head. 'There's no denying you, missus. I'll try a bit.' George always demolished what was on the plate and Mum would tell the grinning Mary 'You see. I told you he was hungry.'

For lunch George would sit down in the kitchen and eat doorstop cheese and beetroot sandwiches and fruit. He would down three or four large cups of tea and then go back to work. Within the hour Mum would take him out a tray of tea and biscuits and George would look helplessly at the smiling Mary.

'He was hungry,' Mum would excuse her actions.

'Of course . . .'

When Mum died unexpectedly of a burst appendix after the war George turned up as usual. It was his day to do our garden. He arrived 30 minutes before we were due to set off in the funeral procession. The hearse and cars were lined up outside. George did not know that Mum had even been ill or taken to hospital, let alone dead. He wore a bowler hat which he always took off when he came into the house. When he edged tentatively through the mourners, all the men wearing hats, he was at a complete loss. Rose took his arm and led him into the privacy of the kitchen and told him Mum was dead. George was stunned. He looked out at the geraniums and tears trickled down his weather-beaten face. He was unashamedly grieving. Rose, grieving herself, left him. Mick went to see George, and he said, 'If you want to come to the funeral, George, we'll find a seat in the car for you. It's at the Jewish cemetery in Edmonton. We'll bring you back here when it's over.'

George shook his head, unable to speak. Then, he said, 'I won't go. I couldn't bear it. I'd just like a last walk in the garden, if that's all right.'

Mick nodded. George went out into the garden and looked down at Mum's favourite geranium bed. Force of habit made him stoop and straighten this out and adjust that. Just before the cortege departed Rose went out to see George. He handed her a small bunch of greenery, with a centrepiece of three geraniums, a red, a white and a pink. He had neatly tied it together with string. He gave it to Rose and said, 'A favour, Miss Rose. Put this on your mother's grave for me. Would you?'

That was impossible. Flowers were not allowed on graves in orthodox Jewish cemeteries. It was inadmissible. Rose knew this, but she said, 'I'll do that, George.' She took the bouquet from him and when the cortege reached the cemetery Rose stopped the car by the gates, alighted and placed George's tribute against the wall.

George never came back to the house again. He was truly a natural gentleman in every sense of the word. The garden went to rack and ruin.

The mid-1930s saw the chasm between immigrant parents and their British-born sons, more so than daughters, widen so far that reconciliation became impossible. Affected by the mores of the more tolerant English culture, the new generation balked at being told to believe in what they did not believe in. Very often attempts at honest argument ended in lost tempers and parental heartbreak. The new generation had been too well educated just to acquiesce. The immigrant elders like Dad were too fundamentalist to allow themselves even the merest grain of flexibility or compromise. It was truly a perfect example of the immovable object meeting the irresistible force.

Bad experience and lingering memories had eroded Dad's trust in Christian behaviour. The anti-Semitism being whipped up by Mosley's blackshirts underlined his feelings. But we, his sons, who studied with gentiles, played games with them and counted quite a few as friends rejected our elders' beliefs as bigotry. 'This is England,' we would say, 'not Russia or Poland.' To which our parents would reply

> Oh, yes? Look at the German Jews. They thought they were safe and secure. They were more German than Jewish. Now, see what is happening to them. Take the Spanish Jews before the Inquisition. They thought they had well integrated, and they had . . .

Put simply, Dad and his contemporaries regarded themselves as Jews. Their religion was their nationality. On the other hand their children regarded themselves as Englishmen who happened to be of the Jewish faith. Looking back I can see that Dad's views expressed a deeply-embedded anger at the generations of Jews who had been cats'-pawed by Europe's envious peasantry and intellectual opportunists. Contrary to our parents' views, all that was Jewish was not always good and all that was not Jewish was not necessarily hostile.

Yet, our fathers tied us long enough to the tap root of the Judaic tree for us never to break free from it. Later, I encountered co-religionists who, when they had faced death, had found themselves spilling out that awesome yet comforting final prayer 'Hear O Israel. The Lord our God, the Lord is one.' And, in Hebrew.

Mick told me he uttered it more than once when the planes he flew across the lethal Arctic wastes spluttered or hit exceptional turbulence. I muttered it several times when bobbing up and down in an open lifeboat after we had been torpedoed just south-west of Iceland when I was on the *MV Hylton*. Men died and were pushed into the very cold seas and we were beginning to accept we would never be found. The corvette *HMS Dianella*, making a final search for survivors, chanced upon us. When I reached home after that Dad rushed me to Shacklewell Lane synagogue for a special prayer thanking God for my survival. Judaism has a prayer for every human eventuality. A young sergeant pilot shared the *bima* with me. He had baled out from a burning Hurricane over the Channel. Yes, he remembered screaming and swearing as he struggled to get free of the plane and, yes, he thought he had included that *Shema Yisroel* prayer.

The advance of time brought tangible changes and in the late 1930s small businesses started by immigrants had developed into sizeable companies and a few had even gone public and had become household names. I kept hearing about boys and girls I knew who had made it to Oxford and Cambridge. Sometimes, one of Dad's friends, looking like a cat that has swallowed the cream, boasted of a son who had qualified in this or that profession. Some had made it into the big bands. Others had passed through the Royal Academy of Music and were playing with reputable philharmonic orchestras. A boy in Sandringham Road had become an apprentice with a shipping company. He caused quite a stir when he came to synagogue in his cadet's uniform. The British-born Jews were busily climbing upwards and outwards in every direction.

For those of us who were not so ambitious or academically inclined there was a wealth of siren distractions. Sam and Rose had graduated to more adult pursuits like dancing at the Hammersmith Palais and The Astoria. Rose loved the bright lights and the dancing and was always being collected by boys. Mary once remarked, 'Your sister Rose is a real smasher.'

'Where?' queried Aubrey. 'I can't see it.' To which Mary said that Aubrey could not see beyond the end of his nose unless food was involved.

Dad was not too happy at Rose's frivolity but so long as the boys were Jewish he accepted them. Now and again Rose would bring a boy home. Despite being made welcome the boys were often very apprehensive, as if they felt a trap being sprung on them. If Mary disapproved of a boy she would say 'I wouldn't give that one two halfpennies for a penny.'

Rose would laugh. Freda, quieter, more introvert and less confident, seldom went out. Occasionally, Rose would haul her into making a foursome, occasions that were not too successful.

Mid-teenagers had the clubs, meccas of entertainment where one could participate freely in a wide range of activities covering all sports, music, literature, chess and various educational projects. There were gymnasiums with boxing squares, wrestling mats and a vaulting horse and high bars, rings and ropes to climb. The clubs were noisy friendly places where no one whispered and boys and girls seemed to dash hither and thither non-stop.

Spare evening? Nothing to do? Off to the club. Most of us

had the same background; immigrant parents, attendance first at elementary and then on to grammar and secondary schools. We all had the same strict upbringing. Please! Thank you! Sorry! I beg your pardon! were often heard and automatically uttered. Boys stood up to give the female sex chairs and seats in buses and opened doors for them. This did not preclude high spirits and larking about. Graffiti and vandalism were unheard of.

Inevitably, it was at the clubs that boys first became aware that girls offered delights other than those to be found on playing fields. The first gauche fumblings and embarrassments led many to vow that never again would he make such a damned fool of himself. But, natural forces prevailed. Boys gravitated towards girls and vice versa, and boisterous mixed circles dared to say things which at home would have earned them sharp clips around the head. Then came the exhilaration of the pairing off with the new infatuation. New emotions of jealousy and noses being put out of joint taught sharp lessons. To the victors went the elation of the triumphant.

Sophistication was rare. In our close coterie it existed in the shape of Norman, the dapper cheeky chappie with the large expressive black eyes and unruly shock of black hair. One evening we were gazing at a pretty blonde girl whose shapely legs turned more heads than the photographs of Zionist pioneers on the walls. She was reading a book and was totally engrossed in it.

'There,' explained Norman, the self-appointed expert, 'is a girl with class.'

'Too classy for you, mate,' said Max.

'She'll never fall, not even for your charm, Norman,' said Issy.

'She can't fall for what he hasn't got,' snorted Max. 'She'll probably strangle him with the daft cream silk scarf he wears around his neck and I'd gladly pull one end of it.'

Norman well knew he was being dared to try his luck. He

did not take all that encouraging. Mortally afraid of campsite earwigs he may have been, but when it came to braving girls he was a lionheart. He said, 'If I get to talk to her, what is it worth?'

'Bugger all,' said Max, 'and don't grin.' Here Max had a point. Norman did possess a very wide cheshire cat grin that you wanted to throw things at.

Issay, eyeing the girl judiciously, said, 'No, Max. If he succeeds we'll buy him a coffee and piece of cake.'

'Done.'

How we all envied Norman's fearless panache as he walked straight over and perched himself on the girl's armchair. She was surprised. She frowned. She moved away from Norman. She said something and from her expression it was not welcoming.

'Aye, aye,' observed Max happily, 'he'll soon be back.'

Max was wrong. We watched Norman dripping Hollywood charm by the bucketful and smiling widely as he gently took the book from the girl. He looked at it intently and then had a very intense conversation about it with the girl. They both became very animated. We fell silent. I heard Max mutter that he would be buggered more than once. Then, grinning from ear to ear, Norman came back to us and said, 'Make it two coffees and cakes. Sonia is joining me.'

'How did you do it?' asked Issy, scientifically curious.

'Personality.' Norman tapped the side of his nose with his index finger. 'Some have it. Others haven't.'

'I've always said that girls are stupid cows,' said Max. 'This confirms it.'

Later, Norman told me the secret of his success. The book was *Magnolia Street*, by Louis Golding. So, Norman said to Sonia, 'That's my uncle. He writes well, doesn't he?'

That did not break the ice. It shattered it. Norman dated his conquest. They went to the cinema and over Hackney Downs after dusk and Norman had never looked so pleased with himself. When questioned about his fortune, or lack of it, under the spreading oaks, he would look infuriatingly smug and tut-tut 'Gentlemen never talk about their lady friends'.

Norman had devastated Sonia's defence by telling her that he would get her book autographed by his uncle, the author. Having lied, he had the problem of how to fulfil his promise. When it came to girls Norman was ever resourceful. He gained time by telling her that the book would have to be posted and then returned from Manchester. She understood. Eight days later Norman handed the book back to Sonia. The inscription on the fly leaf read 'To Sonia, my nephew Norman's close friend. I do hope that you enjoyed reading the story, yours very sincerely, Louis Golding'.

Issy and Max remained confounded by Sonia's warmth towards Norman. They never knew about the inscription. I never told them. Because, ground down by Norman's persuasive pleading, I wrote and signed it. Did it help? I asked him.

'Help?' Norman put his arm around my shoulder. 'Boy, did it help.' Qualms never troubled Norman. I felt uneasy about the deception, especially when I spoke to Sonia. Norman was more pragmatic. 'Think of the tremendous pleasure you've given her,' he said. 'She'll never know it wasn't Louis Golding who wrote on that fly-leaf.'

Then, virgins until marriage were the rule rather than the exception. Most girls enjoyed a kiss and a spot of heavy petting but, generally, that was as far as it went. The few who went the whole hog became known to all. Not wishing to damage their standing with other girls at the club, boys tended to give them a wide berth. On the club premises, of course.

Whereas Norman was extrovert, even flaunting, Issy was discretion itself, but in no way less effective. When in the middle of a hectic evening Issy was nowhere to be seen we would study the girls and wonder which one he had squirreled away to a more private spot. When taxed about it later he would reply quietly, 'Girls? What girls? I'm too busy studying to waste time on Normanising.'

At the *Habonim* camps Issy would slip away after the evening meal to keep a pre-arranged rendezvous. His return during the early hours, disturbing yet again a disgruntled Berl, exuded all the deep satisfaction of a fulfilled tom-cat.

Max regarded girls as noisy, demanding, brainless buggers and a waste of money. I cannot recollect him ever having taken one out. He was personable enough, blonde-haired with blue eyes and a sturdy figure, if a bit short in the legs. I wondered sometimes whether he had ever slept with a woman before he was killed over the North Sea.

Berl went out with a merry dumpy soprano who sang in the same operatic company as he did. At parties she plumped onto his lap and stayed there. When they sang duets accompanied by a pianist they did command attentive appreciative audiences. Norman observed kindly, 'They're just made for one another.'

'They are,' agreed Max, adding lugubriously, 'the poor sods.' We all found Max's misogyny a great source of enjoyment.

Both Sam and Mick were going out with a succession of girls and when they wanted to economise they would bring them home for refreshments. The Jewish dates, of course. Later, Mum and Mary would relax and exchange views about the girls. Girls regarded as being hot stuff were never brought home.

What the elders feared most of all was intermarriage – the threat of their children marrying outside the faith. When this happened the most uncompromising of fathers literally regarded their sons as being dead and did not want to see or hear from them again. To them, it was the ultimate betrayal. For the families involved those were harrowing sackcloth and ashes times. Yet, while the fathers may have enjoyed the pyrrhic satisfaction of feeling that they were the true upholders of Judaism, it was always the mothers who grieved the most about a split family. Aware of this many errant sons maintained

151

a clandestine contact with their mothers. I cannot recollect one Jewish mother or sister who went along with the sharp cut of excommunication.

There was the undeniable attraction of opposites. Many gentile girls expressed preference for Jewish boys. They found us different, but in the best of ways, not like the horned and tailed miserable creatures depicted in anti-Semitic cartoons and literature. If a Jewish boy succumbed to appetite and invitation and had sex with a Jewish girl, his upbringing made him feel terribly guilty. Facing the girl's parents, even though they knew nothing about it, in the street or synagogue, chilled stomachs and jellied knees.

'It's terrible,' discussed one notorious sower of wild oats. 'When you poke a Jewish girl you feel such a rotten sod. You are so ashamed of yourself, you wish you hadn't done it. You vow never to touch her again. Then, at the club, she'll come over to you and it's away to the races once more.'

These sexual activities necessitated the purchase of condoms, known then, colloquially, as French letters. They were a taboo subject, never to be mentioned or talked about. Adolescent boys discussed them furtively and never in mixed company. There were no sex lessons in schools. One learned the mechanics of reproduction by trial and error and the thrill of discovery. It was always intoxicating to anticipate what new delights were around the corner.

Very few chemist shops dared sell condoms. Chains like Boots would not stock them. Barber shops were the main vendors. The tiny packets of Durex would nestle behind the arrays of scent and shampoo bottles and when a customer asked for a 'you-know-what' Harry with a wink would slide his hand behind the bottles, enclose the packet inside a clenched fist and slide it quickly into the customer's hand. The customer, looking around furtively to see if anyone had noticed, would surreptitiously draw his hand under the coverall gown and slide it into a pocket.

Buying a condom then was very much a cloak and dagger operation. Many a boy who looked forward to his first date with great expectations did not fulfil them because he could not pluck up the courage to ask the barber he had been visiting for years for a packet of Durex. A few chemist shops did sell them. There were boys who knew them and who, for a small fee, would go into them and buy the required packets for others. Other boys would gird their loins, march bravely into the chemist for the Durex and then emerge with toothpaste or a packet of soap. It was a hard life for the innocent.

Strangely, even though many in their late teens had reached an understanding with their fathers that they would go to the Sabbath morning services only if they felt like it, many kept up the habit. We still found the services too repetitious and boring but at the Stoke Newington synagogue we were lucky enough to have had a Rabbi Harris Cohen as minister. He had a comfortable sense of humour and was approachable in contrast to other humourless even pompous guardians of the faith. He was a short energetic man with a trimmed Van Dyke beard. He spoke perfect English and his diction was stage perfect. His antennae were well tuned into the desires of all ages of his congregation and he knew all about the fanaticism of his younger congregants for football. One Saturday afternoon a big local derby came round. Tottenham were playing Arsenal in an important top of the table match. The kick-off was scheduled for 2.30 p.m. That morning you could sense the restlessness in the synagogue. Only on *Yom Kippur* have I seen watches studied so often and intently. At 12.15 p.m. Rabbi Harris Cohen mounted the pulpit for his weekly sermon. The tension was palpable. How long would he speak for. He smiled around at his flock and said, 'I suppose I suffer from the rabbinical weakness of talking too much to congregants who never listen. Well, that's what I'm paid to do. However, even rabbis are human and today I suffer from a very sore throat so I will make this a very short sermon indeed.'

153

He kept his word. The sermon was over in five minutes. One could almost hear the muffled cheer that went up at the goal Rabbi Harris Cohen had just scored. The elders were puzzled. The rabbi's voice had sounded strong and clear to them. With football supporters his stock soared high although Issy's elder brother Harry said cynically, 'I'll bet he's got a ticket for the game himself.'

After the service and the shaking of hands and wishing everyone in sight a Good Sabbath we all raced home. Everyone was talking about getting to the game early. Except me. I would have given my right arm to have gone to the match but that afternoon I was playing for the school at Lower Edmonton. Issy waved his ticket under my nose, and teased, 'Nothing in life is perfect.'

Chapter Thirteen

The gentle smell of war emanating from the continent and pervading the atmosphere of the late mid-1930s grew stronger and stronger. With the carnage of the 1914–18 war within recent memory it was universally accepted that only the most evil of maniacs would precipitate another one. Yet, such a man had surfaced in Germany. Warnings by the few realists that the threat of war was alive and growing and that the country should re-arm were pooh-poohed, even sabotaged, by Hitler's too many admirers. The apprehensive lick-spittled the strong and Hitler's British running dogs were Mosley's British Union of Fascists and Arnold Leese's Imperial Fascist League.

They copied everything about the Nazis; their creed, their uniforms, their salutes, their slogans, their tactics, their contempt for democracy and their brutality. Above all they plugged the race hatred card to successfully win support.

Sporadic skirmishes between fascists and anti-fascists in Hackney increased. An anti-Semitic remark in school and a Jewish boy, if he felt strong enough and angry enough, would catch his tormentor outside the gates and the fists would fly. More Jewish shop windows were daubed and smashed. Anti-Semitic graffiti abounded to the point where it became an accepted part of the everyday scene. The Jews were too few and lacked a strong lead from their communal leaders. As a result, quite a few of the more hot-headed young Jews grew fed up with keeping a low profile and joined the communists purely because the communist party were the only ones attempting to take the fight to the fascists. This fact, fanned by fascist propaganda, created the myth that all Jews were communists. Really, it was remarkable how very few Jews, given the fascist provocation, joined the communist party.

There were more fascist meetings and they appeared in new places. They used loud-speaker vans which flew the Union Jack and the fascist flag. They always had police protection and it was infuriating to stand helplessly outside the perimeter of a crowd and listen to their speakers slagging off Ikey Moes or the Yids with the most outrageous of calumnies. It was even more agonising to see the attentive crowd actually drinking in the words. As the meetings were always salted with fascist heavies one could either listen quietly or walk away. As Issy and I and a restless Max listened to fascist speakers in Church Street, Stoke Newington, Issy grabbed Max's arm and warned, 'That's a mincing machine. Cause trouble and you'll end up in small pieces.'

'Maybe we should join the communists,' I said.

Issy shook his head. 'Save your fire for the only solution, Zionism.'

Although the fascists regarded the Jews as a docile frightened minority only wanting to avoid trouble they were wary of the exceptions, like the notorious Gold brothers, tough compact street fighters in every sense of the word. They went out after dark with like-minded others and hunted for fascists. They did not mind tackling a few over the top but where they were hopelessly outnumbered they avoided a fight.

The fact was that there were too many fascists and their supporters and too few Jews. Which is why the fascists always held the high ground. If they wanted to march provocatively through a Jewish area or hold a meeting adjacent to a synagogue on a Friday evening they could do so, shielded by scores of tough stewards and police protection. Anti-fascists who heckled or threw punches were arrested for causing a breach of the peace. Frustrations produced hair-brained schemes and I became involved in one that at first sight seemed to be a brilliant idea.

'Catapults,' said Lenny to a group of us in the school playground. 'Just like David used against Goliath.'

Catapults could be bought in many shops. Put a stone in the pad, pull back the elastic to full stretch, aim, release grip on the pad and the stone would fly with great velocity a surprisingly long distance. Ten of us who decided to take part each bought a catapult.

Early mornings and late evening when few people were about we practised over Hackney Downs. We began by aiming at trees and went on to aiming at cardboard apple boxes. Roundish stones about three-quarters of an inch in diameter made the best missiles. It was surprising how accurate some of us became. At 20 yards we were hitting the apple boxes time and again and we felt very confident that some of our shots would hit targeted fascist speakers. We were so intoxicated with excitement that any gnawing doubts as to the wisdom of what we had embarked upon were easily suppressed.

Issy advised strongly against our intention. Norman, with girls occupying so much of his spare time, thought we were crazy. Max was one of us. Being Max he grumbled about the bloody stupidity of the scheme, at his own crass idiocy at having wasted four pennies on a catapult and at the general daftness of it all.

The ten of us were Lenny, a quiet slim boy who passed Matriculation with distinctions and later won a state scholarship to Cambridge, Max, myself and three others from The Grocers school named Sidney, Harold and Ivor. Stephen and Adam went to Latymer Grammar and the other two were the two Gold brothers. When they accosted me in Amhurst Road, where they lived, and said they wanted to take part I could hardly refuse. Besides, if it came to a fight they were definitely the ones to have on your side. They were rough, tough and hard just like their father, a fearsome man.

He was tall and wide with bulging muscles and a triangular face. He had piggy black eyes deeply set in a tightly stretched leathery skin. He worked with horses in a Brick Lane brewery. There was not an ounce of spare flesh on him. If you shook hands with him you needed to hold your own hand under the running cold water tap to ease the pain of the grip. It was not sadism. He just did not know his own strength. He was a devout man and attended the Dalston Talmud Torah on the Sabbath and yet it was rumoured that he ate *trefa*, non-kosher meat. If this were true it was a terrible sin. Everyone was curious about it but no one dared ask Mr Gold to his face about it.

The two Golds apart, the rest of us on the catapult scheme were callow schoolboys and yet streetwise, even if we turned crimson at the drop of a genitalic word in front of girls. Macho was a word we had never heard of. What we decided to do stemmed from shame at our overall communal inactivity. We kicked against being pressed to keep a low profile in the face of incessant provocation. The Golds, on the other hand, were older than we were and they went out to work. This gave them a maturity and self-confidence that we lacked. Both had gone straight from elementary school into work. Danny worked in a bakery and his brother heaved heavy bolts of fabric about in a warehouse.

On a very few occasions I went out with the Golds and their gang on one of their after dark forays. It was comforting to be with half a dozen or so boys all as hard and tough as the Golds. I was surprised to learn that the gang and the fascists knew each other, even by first name terms. The game had a set of rules. If the Gold gang passed fascists on opposite pavements there would be verbal abuse aplenty, but that was all. When the Gold gang encountered fascists on the same pavement neither side would give way, then we moved through one another in what can only be described as a few moments of high voltage tension. If no one jostled both sides continued peacefully on their way. If there was one push, blow or kick then fighting would break out. And it would be savage.

Back to the catapults. Having bought them and trained with them we itched to use them. So one evening eight of us met at Lenny's house to discuss the next stage. The Golds said they would turn up on the night. Lenny's father was a fruit importer and wholesaler and he owned a large detached house with certainly an acre of garden at the back. The half next to the house was lawn and flower beds. The back half was an orchard with plum, pear, apple and cherry trees. It even had a mirabelle with a crop of golden luscious plums. Munching fruit that we picked we settled down to work out our plan.

We decided to target one of the meetings held at the top of Ridley Road where a perfect forum was provided where the road widened as it debouched into Kingsland High Street. The advantage for us was the number of escape routes leading away from the site. There was Kingsland High Street itself, running two ways, with two streets opposite giving escape routes towards Newington Green. Twenty yards down from the High Street was an alleyway leading straight into Sandringham Road. Further down still was the curving Colveston Crescent, which led down past the majestic St. Marks Church. The other side of the forum presented two more exits leading into Dalston Lane.

Len said, 'That's settled the target and the escape routes. Now what next?'

Silence. Then Max said, 'Forget the whole silly idea. Who wants a catapult? They can have it for half price.'

'Got the wind up?' exclaimed Ivor.

'No. Just the first to come to his senses.'

The expressions of outrage were not echoed by all those present. It was not cowardice but the dawning of a new light.

159

Stephen said, 'Supposing we hit an innocent bystander?'

'Serves the bugger right for being there,' said Max.

'What happens if we hit a policeman?' asked Adam.

'Then,' said Max cheerfully, 'they'll put you in prison and throw away the key.'

The argument raged as we munched the fruits we had picked. Lenny listened quietly to us all and then he raised his hand for silence and said, 'Right. Those who want to pull out must do so now. No hard feelings . . .'

'Let's forget the catapults,' blurted Ivor. 'Let's go to a meeting with the Golds and just clobber every blackshirt in sight.'

'Brilliant,' snorted Max. 'There would be a need for ten stretchers and we'd be on them.'

We took a five-minute break, strolling among the trees and collecting our thoughts before we regrouped in a cricle. Stephen, Adam and Sidney had plucked up the courage to drop out. They were shamefaced about it. We told them that it was all right, no sweat, no worry. But it was. Not only did we regret the loss of firepower but we envied them the courage to have pulled out. I was more cowardly. I would sooner have faced a thousand blackshirts than the scorn of those left. Much later I learned that they all felt the same way.

We fixed a meeting for the following week to decide which meeting to attack and operational details. The raid, or lunacy as Max referred to it, took over our lives. At home, in school, on the playing fields, in bed and sitting next to Dad in synagogue. The ever sharp Mary noticed my distraction and tried to worm the cause of it out of me. She tried to bribe me with the offer of one of her superb cakes, even a chocolate sponge. Even this failed.

Harold dropped out. He had told his sister about it. She was horrified and told their father. He told his son that if he did not drop out of the scheme he would never be a threat to the fascists because he, his father, would personally break his neck. He told his son to advise us all not to go through with it.

Down to six. Nevertheless, Ivor, Lenny, Max and I held the arranged meeting. The Golds said they would turn up on the night. We accumulated a sufficient store of stones to give us ten each. Lenny said that it would have to be a let fly and run operation. 'With the accent on the run,' commented Ivor.

Although the blackshirts were holding regular weekly meetings in Stamford Hill, Upper Street, Islington, Clapton Common, Hertford Street, Amhurst Road and elsewhere, we decided to stick with Ridley Road. The quietly efficient Lenny had made six copies of a sketch map of Ridley Road and its environs. On them, he had marked out vantage points from where we could unleash our fusillades and red lines to indicate the escape runs we should take. He had even noted the closest bus stops so that if we were lucky and coincided with a bus at a stop we could jump on it. We would each fire a rapid four stones at least and then beat it. It would be a case of *sauve qui peut*. And if we were caught? 'Don't even think about it,' advised Lenny.

Fascist meetings started around 7 o'clock. Warm up speakers, apprentices in the trade of race hatred, would man the platform and speak to planted bystanders. Passers-by would gather around them. More people attracted more people. The crowd would build up for the main speakers in the evening, usually two, who were experienced and plausible orators. Their themes were always the same; the rottenness of democracy and the need to replace it with a strong leadership, Britain for the British, patriotism to the nth degree and the preservation of Anglo-Saxon racial purity which necessitated deportation of all Jews. Racial incitement and being mealy-mouthed did not go together. Where the German Nazis trod, the British fascists loped along behind. We chose a Thursday evening for our attack.

Monday. Four days to go. My unease showed. Rose grabbed me and demanded 'Come on, brother. What's eating you?' Rose, shrewd and loaded with common sense, had developed into the family trouble-shooter and pourer-of-oil. When Dad, together with Mick and Sam, discussed business, which always resulted in raised angry voices because times were hard and nerves stretched to breaking point, it was Rose who either led a distressed Mum up to her bedroom or bearded the dining room and stopped the quarrelling. She persisted with me but I held my silence.

Tuesday morning Max buttonholed me in the school playground and said 'You're down to five'.

'Who has fallen out?'

'Me.' Max looked defiantly ashamed. 'I'm sorry. My sister Nin wormed it out of me. She pinned me down for over an hour until I promised to duck out.'

'Come on, Max. No one can make you do what you don't want to do.'

It was the only time I had ever seen Max squirm with embarrassment. He said 'To be honest, I've been thinking about it and nothing else. We'll shoot a few stones and cause maybe a tiny bit of disruption. So what? If we get caught we'll be beaten and kicked to pieces and probably go to prison. And, what for?' For the rest of the break he pinned me against a wall and implored me to drop out as well.

Well, that was that. After school I walked home in a light rainfall with Lenny. He was not surprised that Max had fallen out. It was probably the sensible thing to do.

'But, you were all for it,' I protested.

Lenny shrugged. 'I was. Like you, I just wanted to hit back at the bastards. It was a relief to think of doing something, anything. But it was a bit crazy. Let's tell Ivor.'

We called at his house in Kenninghall Road. Ivor was having his tea. His mother offered us a meal, which we declined. Ivor was a bit of a tearaway and always keen to have a go. He stood with us outside in the street and we told him it was off. He just said 'Now, I've got my appetite back. I'm going back in to clear all the plates.'

After I had eaten supper, watched by Mary who noticed the change in me, I met Lenny. We called at the Golds. They both listened to us as we told them it was off. They took it stoically enough, then Danny said 'I'm not going to waste the money I spent on the catapult.' We advised caution. Danny just grinned and said 'Caution? What's that?'

I returned to normal. I slept soundly at night and ate heartily. Mary observed that I looked as if I had lost a farthing and found a shilling. The episode taught me a valuable lesson, never to start what I knew I would never be able to finish.

The Clarfelts bought a goat and kept it in their back garden. No one knew why they did so. The goat was not there to provide milk. They had in a gardener once a week who mowed the lawn. The goat played havoc with the flower beds and covered the garden with droppings. Our neighbourhood feral cats sat on the wall surrounding the garden and stared down curiously at this strange animal. They were cautious enough to stay out of its reach. Clarfelt's two neighbours, Dad and Mr Galinsky, agreed that it was a madness. But England was a free country and if Old Man Clarfelt wanted to keep a goat, so be it.

At one spot in the common brick wall between our gardens there was a gap down to waist level. The July day was hot. All doors and windows in our house were open. Mum was out at the cinema with her friends. Mary was up in her room. Everyone else was out. Dad came home earlier than usual. He went up to his bedroom to take off his jacket, stiff collar and tie, and he came face to face with the goat. Mary said later that his yell nearly made her fall out of her open bedroom window. A petrified Mrs Stark locked herself in her rooms and kept calling out in panic, 'What happened? Is anyone hurt?

Dad recovered from his shock and hurtled next door to bang furiously at the Clarfelts' street door. It was opened by George, the youngest son, tall, lanky easy-going George.

'Your goat' exploded Dad, 'is in my bedroom!'

'How?' George was dazed. 'How did it get there?'

'You tell me,' said Dad. 'Now come and get it out'.

George followed Dad into our house and into the bedroom and straight into another crisis. The goat had jumped onto the bed and, making the most of its unbelievably good fortune, was rolling and rubbing itself over the eiderdown which was looking distinctly the worse for wear. Feathers were escaping from tears in the fabric and were floating about the room. George grabbed the goat. The goat resisted. It was not going to give up its new found comfort without a fight. The eiderdown deteriorated fast before Dad's very eyes. He put his hands to his head and walked out, muttering 'Just get it out'.

Aided by Mary, George pushed and pulled the stubborn animal down the front steps of our house and through the Clarfelt's house and back into their garden. The next day the Clarfelts had covered the gap with wire netting. Mary made Dad a strong cup of tea as the plaintive voice of Mrs Stark continued to float down from her beleagured flat.

'Please, will someone tell me what has happened?'

Dad suddenly laughed. 'Go on Mary,' he said. 'Put her out of her misery.'

Everyone had a good laugh about it. Old Man Clarfelt insisted upon buying Mum a new eiderdown. For days after the incident George and I tried to persuade that goat to jump over a hurdle the same height as the gap in the wall. It was perversity personified. It even refused to try. The noisy proceedings were watched with great interest by the cats on the walls.

George was younger than I by about nine months. When war broke out he itched to get into it. In early 1942 I heard that he had enlisted and was in the tank corps. During training he drove his tank into the only electric pylon in a large field and blacked out various habitations on the Salisbury plain for several hours. He was commissioned and posted to a crack Scottish cavalry regiment, the Lothian and Border Horse, so named even though tanks had replaced horses. He went overseas quickly and they fought through North Africa, Sicily and then up through Italy. George wrote me a couple of air letters which I received in Bombay. Piquantly, when he was posted to the regiment his fellow officers took unkindly to a Sassenach intruding in their mess. When they learned that he was Jewish, one said 'Och, weel. That's nae so bad.'

It was the end of 1944 when I met up with George in London. He was convalescing. His right leg was still in a plaster splint from below the knee. He sported a gold wound stripe on his cuff. His unit had seen fairly constant action and George had stayed lucky until north of the River Arno in Tuscany his tank was hit. George was blown out of his turret. Despite wounds in both legs he managed to crawl away just before the tank blew up. He lost his crew. In hospital he was told that infection had set in and that his right leg would have to be amputated above the knee. He kicked up such a tremendous fuss, saying he would sooner lose his life than a leg, that he was one of the first to be treated with that new wonder drug, penicillin. It saved his leg.

George introduced me to a fellow officer, Derek, who was marrying a West Country girl in Somerset. He had asked George to be his best man. Derek told me that George had been regarded as something of a character. The Lothian and Border Horse were often at the very top of the advance and frequently in action. In one fracas George had hung his helmet on the outside of the tank. It had been scarred by two dents from either bullets or shrapnel. The fight over, George had donned his helmet and was sauntering by the colonel when the latter saw the dents and exclaimed, 'Clarfelt. Are you all right?'

'Bit of a headache, sir. That's all.'

'That's the spirit,' enthused the colonel. 'Well done.'

George told me about his sergeant, Douglas, a short wiry Glaswegian who had been no stranger to the inside of Barlinnie prison. When his unit was ordered forward to see if there were any Germans in a hamlet, farm or village, it was at times necessary for someone to go forward on foot to a vantage point with binoculars to assess the situation. George did it and there were times when he sent his sergeant to do it. When the sergeant protested George would point out that as it cost the country more money to train an officer than an NCO his would be the biggest loss to the exchequer.

Douglas had a keen nose for loot. Occasionally, he would slip away into deserted buildings and houses and when he returned he would show George the jewellery and gold and silver items that he had found. He would pucker his sharp-featured face into a gnomic smile and explain that he had to think of the wife and kids.

'You're not married,' said George.

'Och, I know that. But I've got to plan for the future, sir.'

'What about my cut?'

Indignation from the sergeant. 'That, sir, goes without saying.'

'Okay, Douglas. You can carry on with your planning.'

George remembered a Tuscan village nestling between two hills. It was occupied by Germans. Supported by infantry the Lothians cleared the buildings. From a cellar emerged five young members of the Hermann Goering divison. The cellar had held a fine stock for wines and the Nazis were almost arrogant with inebriation. The Jew rose in George and he experienced a great urge to shoot them. Instead he said, 'Search them, Doug.'

The Nazis emptied their pockets and wads of notes, rings, trinkets and necklaces fell to the ground. As Douglas picked them up and put them into a small bag he said with genuine indignation, 'The thieving bastards, sir. Would you believe it?'

George had told the sergeant that when the war was over, if he could find no worthwhile work in Scotland, he could come down to London and contact him. But, Douglas died in that tank.

The very last time George and I went out as friends was right at the end of the war in Europe. We met two girls who were lead dancers in a West End show. George's girl, from Norwich, really fell for George. As the four of us dined together in an Old Compton Street restaurant my companion whispered to me, 'I don't think they know we exist.'

As we slipped away, I said 'See you George.'

He looked up abstractedly. 'Of course. Absolutely.'

166

Our ways diverged. We never went out again. Old Man Clarfelt sold out his massive business for a very large sum and provided plenty for his sons to engage in business ventures, which George did. He married, raised a son and daughter, and for many years lived not far from me in West Hampstead. We seldom met, and then to reminisce about the old days in Hackey. We always had a good laugh about the goat and my father. George died at the age of 62 from a malignant brain tumour. Some deaths of those I know, I accept. With George, there was a terrible sadness.

Chapter Fourteen

On 30 January 1933 Adolf Hitler became Chancellor of Germany and soon afterwards the Nazis released a reign of terror against German Jews. Jewish businesses were boycotted. To ensure the boycott's success Jewish firms were picketed by Nazi thugs. Jews disappeared into concentration camps. Every sphere of human activity received anti-Jewish legislation. On 5 March that same year the Nazi party won the German elections. Jews throughout the world protested and decided to react in the only possible way. They would boycott German goods. The Jews of Hackney determined to play their part.

Thus, one memorable evening, Dad came home in a very portentous mood, and pronounced, 'We will eat half an hour earlier. Some friends are coming round and we are going to have a very important meeting.'

'What about?' asked Sam automatically, not really interested.

'What about?' Dad turned to Sam ferociously. 'What about? Don't you read the newspapers? Don't you listen to the radio? Are you so taken up with chasing girls that you don't know what is happening in Germany?'

The outburst was startling in its bitterness. We ate in a very subdued egg-shell silence.

The men arrived in a bunch, very punctually. They included Mr Cohen, Mr Kramer, Mr Wasser, a Mr Simmons and five others. Dad ushered them into the dining room and shut the door. At half-time Freda and Rose organised a shuttle service of tea and cakes. Aubrey managed to be on hand to help carry the trays and, at the same time, stuff his pockets. When Mary appeared and scolded his wickedness he smartly disappeared out into the street.

When the meeting broke up the men all walked with a spring in their stride. They had found a way to hit back at the hated German Nazis. It was a tonic. The shopkeepers agreed not to stock German goods. The four manufacturers pledged to stop buying any raw materials of German origin. They had all agreed to instruct families and friends not to buy German and to spread the word. The spontaneous boycott was not a great success although it did dent a thriving Anglo-German fur trade. There were too many loopholes and a surprising lack of conviction among many fellow Jews. Many were certain that the Nazis would rescind the anti-Jew legislation.

Although the German menace was still a distant threat to British Jews its poison slopped over into our backyard and boosted the flow of anti-Jewish incidents; wall daubings, posters, the vandalising of al fresco synagogue furniture, molestations, verbal and physical, and instilling fear of going out after dark into the elderly. I remember Dad's anger at the support given by Lord Rothermere in his *Daily Mail* to Mosley and the British Union of Fascists, making him change from the *Daily Mail* to the *Daily Express*. Although Rothermere did break from the fascists in July 1934 because of the anti-Semitism he had already blotted his copy book irrevocably.

Basically, carrying on with normal life was as difficult as trying to enjoy food at a picnic and being discomforted by hovering wasps. The visible manifestations of the grief lurking around the corner for British Jewry lay in the increase in the numbers of outdoor meetings and the provocatively uniformed columns of blackshirts, sometimes led by flags and bands, occurring in Jewish areas. The colour brown and then black became sartorial threats. Issy and I, as was our wont, were listening to an inflammatory fascist meeting in Gore Road, Bethnal Green, to the standard diatribes that the Jews were responsible for all the country's ills, and I said, 'If I had a brick in my hand, I'd throw it.'

'That,' replied Issy firmly, 'would be a bloody silly thing to do. Think clearly. Think of getting our own country.'

'That's your one track mind, again.'

'Maybe,' agreed Issy equably, 'but it's the only track heading in the right direction.'

Autumn 1945. Jewish ex-servicemen returning from the war, believing they had buried fascism forever, were outraged to find that the British Union of Fascists, which had stayed intact underground during the war both inside the internment camps and outside, was emerging again as a political force under the leadership of Sir Oswald Mosley. On street corners his fascist orators would proclaim 'not enough Jews were burned at Belsen'. Something had to be done. I was a founder member of The 43 Group which with ferocity and discipline attacked and utterly destroyed them over a four-year period. Towards the end of this mini war when the post-war fascists were disintegrating and leaving Mosley's Union Movement, many came over to talk with us.

It was then that I was told by several who had been interned as enemies of the state that after Dunkirk, when the incarcerated fascists were convinced that the Nazis would invade and conquer Britain, there were two main topics of excited conversation. These were that they would help their Nazi masters to make Britain Jew-free and get British Jewry onto the cattle trucks bound for gassing and burning in the concentration camps; and that there would be lots of lovely loot left behind by the murdered Jews for them to share out.

These were the same fascists we encountered in the 1930s. We listened to these potential murderers speak, we stood next to them and we may even have played football over Hackney Downs with them.

By 1936 there was a perceptible surge in fascism towards political power. Both fascist newspapers, the *Action* and the *Blackshirt*, were selling at news kiosks and in the newsagents, and there were many indications that support for Mosley was growing. In August of that year word was getting around that the British Union of Fascists were planning a grand tour de force. It was going to be a blockbuster recruiting march with thousands of fascists flying their banners and flags galore and with bands playing patriotic marching songs. It would go right through the Jewish areas of the East End and would strike terror into faint hearts. It would also impress the waverers, the unemployed, the disgruntled, the street boys and the young impressionables into rushing to don the smart girl-pulling Nazi uniforms. Above all, it would show the British electorate that the fascists were a force to be reckoned with and worth voting for in parliamentary and local elections. It was rumoured that the parade would be protected by a massive police presence and every ingredient to make it a major success would be in place.

It was soon learned that the parade was scheduled for 4 October, a Sunday. It created such a buzz that three weeks beforehand it had become a main topic of conversation. Conviction developed that this was going to be a watershed event. If Mosley got away with it, he would do it again and again and again. Come what may, he had to be stopped. At all costs, at any cost. That was the developing mood. Resistance to the Big March, as it was being called, began to stir. The Spanish Republicans fighting Franco's fascists had raised a stirring slogan 'They shall not pass'. It began to appear on East End walls. It was emotive and was soon to be seen bracketing fascist slogans like 'Perish Judah'. Posters appeared. They were worded almost like a call to arms. All anti-fascists, gentiles and Jews, dockers, trade unionists, shopkeepers, white collar workers and many other groups of artisans were raising contingents to help stop the march. Provincial support was promised. There were rumours and counter-rumours. The South Wales miners would be coming. Tyneside ship-workers and steelworkers would be down. And so on and on.

Hospitals had been warned to be on full alert for the day. There was fierce grass roots resentment of the government for not banning the parade with its deliberate provocation of peaceful citizens and of the police for deciding to turn out in such large numbers to protect the fascists. The situation had boiled down to this; if the government and authorities were not going to stop the anti-democratic hate-filled march, then the British people themselves would do it.

The morning of 4 October the East End awakened and wondered what the day would bring. Would the fascists get through? Could it be stopped? There was no other topic of conversation. Throughout the early hours of that morning men had been making their way to where the battle would take place. For that is what it was going to be. All through those early hours the barricades had been going up blocking the entrances to the wide Whitechapel and Commercial Road. Trams were halted. Their drivers walked away from them. Buses were slewed across the road. Their engines were immobilised and the drivers and conductors joined the men lining up at the barricades. Cars, lorries, two large heavy brewers drays, carts, piles of timbers and rubble gave the barricades depth as well as side to side width. Men stopped work to eat sandwiches, drink tea from flasks and smoke. And all the time workmen strengthened the barricades by interlocking its components.

Gerry Ross, who later became councillor and then mayor of Hackney, was there. He recalled that the mood was such that the fascists were beaten even before they got to the East End. They expected resistance but they had no idea of the strength of that resistance. Above all, they could not conceive that over 5,000 police would not be able to get them through.

But that is what happened. Time and again the police

charged the barricades, trying to clear them out of the way. Time and again the anti-fascists fought them off. Plate glass windows were smashed. Vehicles were overturned. Police and anti-fascists were hurt. Many demonstrators were arrested. Others moved in to fill gaps and man the front lines.

The police gave up on clearing a passage through Commercial Road and Whitechapel. They decided to divert the march through Cable Street, closer to the river and running parallel to Commercial Road. They found they had been out-guessed. Cable Street was barricaded. The police, angry with frustration, strenuously tried to clear a passage for the fascist parade which had been halted. But they encountered a resistance so determined and the fighting became so fierce that what happened that day has ever since been known as The Battle of Cable Street. There were many casualties and arrests. Unable to force a passage through Cable Street the police instructed the fascists to call off their march. The massed parade with its silent bands was dismissed. Stung by defeat when earlier they had been so cock-a-hoop the fascists were in a mean mood and that evening there were many ugly clashes between the fascists and their enemies.

As news of the fascist defeat spread from house to house, person to person, a festive air touched the inhabitants of Hackney. Neighbours spilled out into the streets and congregated in congratulatory groups. Mr Cohen came bursting into our back garden, clenched fists raised high like a victorious boxer as he yelled, 'Well, Yossele, we beat the wicked swines . . .'

Dad laughed, 'We didn't. But, yes, Isaac, they were stopped.'

Never again did the fascists attempt such a march.

The following month the wearing of political uniforms was banned under the Public Order Act and on 1 January 1937 all political processions through east London areas were also banned. Both these acts were damaging blows to Mosley's aspirations. Nevertheless, the street meetings, insults and street violence continued.

Aubrey passed his Matriculation, left school and became articled to a firm of chartered accountants. Dad paid the weekly stipend for his apprenticeship. Aware of Dad's struggle with money Aubrey knuckled down to studying hard, determined to pass the required examinations first time. When he tucked himself away in the dining room in the evenings to study it was Mary who saw that he was not disturbed.

Dad always showed Mary the greatest of respect. His requests to her were always preceded by 'Mary, would you mind?' or, 'Mary. If you have the time?' She, in turn, reciprocated. When Dad retired to rest in an armchair in his favourite dining room it was Mary who would scold any of us making a noise. Mary knew everything about us. I once heard her talking to the maid who had replaced Maggie at the Cohens and she was saying, 'Yes, Mr Beckman does have a hard time. Business is always very difficult and he's always having rows with Sam about it. He sees a war coming and he has four sons. Lucky he has his shul and his card evenings to take his mind off of things . . .'

Transcending all, Mary worshipped Mum, an affection which Mum returned in spades. The genuine loving respect between the elderly worn-down Polish Jewess and the lusty young Tynesider of Irish descent shone. No other word could describe it. When we wondered why Mary never paid a visit home Mum forbade us ever to raise the subject. She was so uncharacteristically vehement about it that we never did.

Matriculation. I surprised everyone, especially my masters, by passing with distinction in French. Liking languages I passed in English and German. Nevertheless my school reports continued to be dogged by that red-inked damning phrase 'Could do better'. It always upset Dad who berated me for wasting too much time playing football and cricket. He could have lashed my backside with the cat o' nine tails but I would still have played them.

By 1938 I had grown tall and thin but I always felt very fit.

174

I was picked to play for the representative public schools XI and was told I was the first boy from The Grocers to have been so honoured. We lost by four goals to three against a combined Oxford and Cambridge University XI, played at Enfield Town's stadium. After a game against Latymer Grammar, where we won well, Mr Howe pulled me aside after I was dressed and introduced me to a thick-set man in fawn raincoat and trilby, and he said, 'This gentleman scouts for Tottenham Hotspur. He would like you to have a game in one of their junior elevens.'

'Me? Play professional?'

'Just a looksee,' said the scout. 'You'd have to work at it but I'm sure you could make the grade.'

I rushed home to tell Aubrey about it. He was probably a better footballer than I was. He did not score many goals but he always stood out in a game. His ball control was instinctive. He could trap a high ball and bring it under control and turn on a sixpence all in one movement. He wrong-footed opponents with consummate ease and would meander past player after player before sliding a precision pass to someone in a scoring position. He listened, then smiled, saying he had been offered a trial for West Ham United in his last year at school.

'Why didn't you take it up?'

'For the same reason you won't.'

Of course, Dad would never have gotten over the shame had one of his sons trotted onto a professional football field on the Sabbath. Besides, what struggling immigrant father wanted to see his son enter such a precarious and low paid profession? To my eternal regret I did not accept the offer, if only to see how I performed.

In autumn 1937 I joined the north London branch of the Maccabi sports organisation. It was in Compayne Gardens, West Hampstead in a large clubhouse with every facility for every sport, including a large basement gymnasium. Its membership was swollen by refugees from Germany, Austria and Czechoslovakia. They were allowed free use of all club facilities. They strengthened the club's teams immeasurably. The two Czech world table tennis champions, Bergmann and Varna, now played for Maccabi. They strengthened the gymnastic and track events teams. They added to the boxing and water polo teams. We all blended well. To get to Maccabi from Hackney was always a long haul by us, tube and walking, not to mention getting back home when Mick was not there with his car. It was always worth it. To my great delight I was invited to play in the London Maccabi football first XI.

Seeing my joy, Aubrey put his arm round my shoulder and said, 'You have got in through reputation. Not yours. Mick's and mine. When we play just move away from your markers, because you'll be centre forward, stay onside and I'll feed you.'

It worked out well. Playing in Sunday league football the Maccabi first XI had gone through one season without losing a game and were doing the same again. Half the team played for top amateur clubs like Nunhead, Leytonstone and others on Saturday. We beat the combined Jewish youth clubs and provided nine out of the 11 players when the South of England Maccabi went up to Manchester and trounced the Northern Maccabi. Playing centre forward between my two elder brothers was a dream come true.

Our manager was a wealthy toy manufacturer and importer. His name was George Hyams. He was a lovable monster and a great practical joker. He loved to bring in new joke toys and play tricks with others in Maccabi House. He was the first to import whoopee cushions from America. He placed these in chairs and armchairs everywhere in the club and as no one then even knew that they existed he created tremendous embarrassment and confusion. He was a larger than life volatile man with a prominent beak of a nose between two shrewd twinkling black eyes, surmouned by a completely bald dome. He was a man with unlimited nervous energy and when action had to be taken turned into the proverbial ball of fire. He had two passions: cricket and football. He never played them but he loved to umpire the one and referee the other. He often umpired the Yorkers' cricket matches and in one memorable match against Stanmore he devastated my brother Mick by turning down three loud confident LBW appeals against the same batsman in the same over. The two Stanmore batsmen looked bemused when, at the end of the over, Mick epitomised the most harrowing of Greek tragedies as he confronted George with arms raised to Heaven and the Yorkers' fieldsmen collapsed in helpless laughter.

George was always seeking stronger opposition for the Maccabi football team. He wanted to test us, he said. Then, one day, he cornered five of the team in a corner of the canteen and said triumphantly, 'Boys, I have done it. I've arranged a fixture with the amateur champions of France, a team called Ivry-sur-Seine.' He certainly grabbed our attention. 'Now for the icing on the cake,' beamed George, 'we're going to play the game in Paris.'

From that moment it was all systems go. Every player made arrangements to leave work, studies and, in my case, school, for the planned long weekend. George became a wireworm incarnate. He phoned each of us several times over with instructions and details. At the final meeting in a lounge in Maccabi House he laid down the law. He said, 'Your kit must be washed, ironed and spotless. Tears and holes must be repaired. All boots to have a new set of studs and new white laces.' He looked pointedly at Mick and said, 'The colours of shirts, stockings and shorts obliterated by weeks of not being washed is definitely out. Remember! Not only are you playing for London Maccabi, but you are playing for England.'

The news threw our home into turmoil. Dad was completely nonplussed. Suddenly three of his sons were going off to Paris. His initial reaction was to be against it, which produced an immediate fierce reaction from his sons, his daughters,

Mary and Mum. Dad retreated, but not before voicing his objections. Was the match going to be played on the Sabbath? No, Dad, on the Sunday. What about food? He did not want us to eat non-kosher food. Of course not, we assured him. We would sooner starve, Aubrey said. This, from Aubrey, made him immediately suspicious. Our answers did not really satisfy him but he had been worn down to realise that ultra-orthodox constraints on his sons had worn very thin. Then, he gave me a terrible moment. He said firmly, 'Morris is too young to go to Paris.'

I nearly burst into tears. Aubrey and Mick swore to look after me. What about the money to pay for his trip? Dad was fighting a strong rearguard action. 'I'll contribute,' said Sam, Mick, Aubrey, Rose, Freda and even Mary. Dad retired. I feel it was this Paris trip that brought home to him that his sons had all irrevocably taken wing. He could query. He could disapprove. But, he could no longer enforce the final say. It must have been so hard for him to adjust. His sons never gave it a moment's thought.

Very early on a bitterly cold Friday morning 20 of us joined the boat train at Victoria station. There were 11 players plus two reserves. George Hyams, an enormous bear in his black raglan overcoat and Siberian fox fur hat, was acting like a demented sheepdog. He dashed to and fro with quick long strides keeping tabs on all his team to ensure they did not miss the train. Our chairman, Harvey Sadow, known affectionately as Chai, one of the family that owned the Beautility furniture manufacturing empire, puffed contentedly on his briar pipe as he moved around exchanging pleasantries. He was very rich, very charming, very generous and very popular. There were five supporters coming along for a bibulous and possibly dirty weekend in Paris.

Nineteen of the party were carefree and determined to enjoy it all. The exception was George. He was diving into different compartments and plucking cigarettes from his team's mouths and exclaiming, 'For God's sake, you'll be playing the day after tomorrow. You'll need all your puff.'

As we boarded the boat he handed us each two pills and instructed us to take them to prevent sickness. They went overboard. During the crossing he suffered an urge to see our football kit and see that it was clean and all in order. He encountered such a wall of opposition he gave up the idea, but not before voicing his uneasiness about the state of Mick's kit. Chai, always the emollient force, treated the entire party to drinks at the bar. Before I could speak Mick ordered a tomato juice for me. I was very miffed at that.

Paris. The hotel was The Roblin in Rue Chaveaulagarde, looking out onto that impressive church, La Madeleine. Despite the bitter weather and falling snow the flower market was a feast of hothouse colours. We shared two to a room. My room mate was Julius Mendel, a fast stocky sixth former and the next youngest to myself. We could not get out quickly enough to explore.

George, waiting by the hotel entrance like a human fly trap, collared his players as they shot down the stairs two by two. He gave every pair the same stern lecture.

Now, boys, Chai and I laid on this match through personal contacts. We want you to put on your best show, even though Ivry may well prove too strong for you. So, tonight, early to bed. Tomorrow you can sightsee and then early to bed tomorrow night. After the match on Sunday you can do whatever you like. Is that understood?

'Yes, George,' each pair chorussed as they shot past him. Chai, puffing away on his pipe, just raised his eyes to Heaven. 'And,' George flung after them, 'in bed by ten o'clock tonight. Latest. Is that understood?'

'Yes, George,' would come the reply and Chai would again look upwards and smile.

179

George stared at Chai and said, 'They sound too bloody good to be true.' Chai grinned so broadly he had to take his pipe from his mouth.

I went across to Mick and Aubrey and said, 'I'm going out with Julius. Do you mind?'

'Mind?' said Mick. 'Mind? We see enough of you at home. So, bugger off . . . By the way, do you need some francs?'

Julius and I walked and walked and walked. We ate foot long baguettes filled with egg mayonnaise, and pastries, and drank coffee. It was wonderful for both of us. We returned to the hotel at about 10.30 p.m. to find George pacing round the lobby smouldering himself into a state of stomach ulceration. 'You're the first two back,' he said grimly. 'What did you do? No. Don't tell me. Just go upstairs and sleep.'

Two more pairs had returned by 2 a.m. George gave them a piece of his mind and shooed them up to bed. Chai returned to the hotel at about 3 a.m., puffing on a glowing pipe. Seeing the state George was in he persuaded him to have a very large Remy Martin cognac. Then, he sat George down in one of those deep armchairs that you could sink into. He watched George fall into a deep sleep, then he spoke to the night porter. Francs changed hands. The night porter met the late-comers before they pressed the night bell and had them tiptoe on stockinged feet past George to their rooms.

The next morning George corralled his team in a corner of the lounge and he gave us hell. We had no consciences. We were a disgrace to Maccabi and to King and country. We were this and that and none of it was commendable. The hotel staff were captivated by George's performance as he listed our shortcomings as patriots and gentlemen. He declared that he had arranged dinner at The Roblin that evening at 8.30 p.m. after which there would be no going out as the match was the following day. That evening, after dinner, George took up guard duty. He patrolled the lobby walking round and round in tight circles by the front entrance. Other guests sidled past this large mad Englishman at great speed. With the enthusiastic connivance of hotel staff his team made their way out to the toilet and past it down a corridor and through an emergency exit to the street. As the attractive blonde receptionist put it, it was very dramatic and amusing and she could see why the English deserved their reputation for being, *pardonnez-moi, m'sieur,* a little peculiar.

Sunday. The morning of the match. It was snowing quite heavily and George was up the wall. It was 8 a.m. and when we sat down to a breakfast of croissants and coffee two of the team were missing. They were Jock Cohen and Marzy Morris, left back and left half respectively. George was whizzing upstairs, downstairs, out into the street and back, an explosive mixture of rage, disbelief and despair. It took all of Chai's considerable charm to make him join us and have some coffee. The rest of us kept our heads and demolished the two large mounds of croissants. It was not so funny. Jock and Marzy made a strong left flank and no one fancied turning out without them. I asked Mick where they could be.

'At an all night cinema,' he said edgily. 'Now, shut up and just eat.'

At 10 a.m. they turned up, as large as life, smoking strong cheroots and not the least bit abashed. George, sunk into a lobby armchair, saw them arrive. His large hands gripped the armrests so tightly we expected to see chunks of leather and horsehair being torn out. Only Bob Shilling saw the smoke coming from his nostrils but we all saw his bushy eyebrows quiver. Chai and two players fell on top of George and held him down in the chair.

'Have a good time, boys?' snarled George, dripping with venom.

'Yes, thanks,' replied Marzy cheerfully.

'Feeling fit for the match?'

'Never better,' said Jock and seeing Chai jerking his head at them like mad they both ran up the stairs. The two players got up, leaving Chai to grip George's arms and talk to him with great intensity. Chai eventually sighed and stood up. George, released, just sat in the chair. He said with such heartfelt resignation that we all felt sorry for him. 'Well, I've done my best.' His voice climbed. He thumped the armrests with clenched fists and vowed, 'But, if they're clapped out before 90 minutes I'll have their guts for garters.'

France, then, had a very large Communist Party. The industrial area of Ivry was one of its strongholds. As the coach took us along through the easing snowfall and streets of drab terraced houses and factories and warehouses we saw many brick and concrete walls daubed with hammers and sickles and slogans supporting the Spanish Republicans. Anti-fascist slogans proliferated.

By the time we reached the stadium the snow had stopped. It was bitterly cold and none of us looked forward to changing into shorts and a shirt. The stadium was called Stade Lenin and we were told that it could hold 30,000 spectators. The game had been publicised by the local press and wall posters. We were gratified to see queues of spectators passing through the turnstiles. When curiosity took us out onto the pitch before we changed we saw Union Jacks, Tricolours and Red Flags flying everywhere. Chai told us that Maurice Thorez, the French Communist Party leader and a member of the French parliament, would be at the game. As we changed in the unheated dressing room George stamped to and fro, pepping us up.

'Remember what's at stake,' he hammered home. 'The honour of London Maccabi and England . . . Thank God, you've got clean gear Mick. It's an acceptable miracle. Keep your heads. Play your normal game. They'll play typical continental football, skilful, well-controlled and on the ground. But, they hate physical contact and hard tackling. So, close them down quickly . . .'

'We would if we had snowshoes,' said Bob Shilling.

182

The occasion was getting to us. Jokes ceased. I was too tense to talk. No one spoke. Some were running on the spot to keep warm. Others engaged in the most peculiar exercises to limber up. Chai came in to tell us that the snow was four inches deep so dribbling would be difficult. He then ushered our supporters out of the dressing room. George put on his fur hat, adjusted his tie, donned black gloves to match his coat, squared his shoulders, opened the door and said, 'Now, lads, follow me. Shoulders back. Heads high. Don't show any sign of freezing. And remember . . .'

'Maccabi and bloody country,' we sang out.

Out on the field my body turned to instant gooseflesh. God, it was cold. The French players were suffering, too. As we lined up for photographers we froze in both senses of the word. The band played *God Save The King*, *The Marseillaise* and *The Internationale*. This latter anthem was sung with great gusto by the crowd, an estimated 15,000.

When the game started both teams dashed about like crazy for the first five minutes, just to get warm, never mind the ball. The Ivry team were skilful. Their control was good. Their passing was accurate. They were very keen to win and beat an English side and they made us look slow and clumsy. This had never happened to a London Maccabi side and we felt very frustrated. At half time they deservedly led by two goals to nil.

Back in the dressing room we faced a rampaging George as we sipped hot cups of tea organised by the ever dependable Chai. Banging his right fist into his left hand he emphasised each point.

'You won't get into the game if you bloody pussy around. You've got to get possession of the ball. That's why they're beating you.'

'It's difficult,' said Mick, 'they keep passing backwards. We've never come across that before . . .'

'They only do that,' snorted George, 'because you stand

183

around like a lot of poofters watching them do it. You've got to harass them into making bad passes. Put them off their game. Throw them out of their stride.'

'How?' asked Jock Cohen.

'By getting a bloody good night's sleep before the game, that's how,' snapped George, still rankled by the morning's episode. 'You've got to stop being bloody polite English gentlemen. You've got to run at them, tackle them, slide them, give them no time to stand on the ball and wave to their bloody friends in the crowd. The moment one of them gets the ball, go at him. If he passes, keep going after that ball. And if that second player passes, keep after that ball. Harry them. They'll get nervous and will soon make mistakes.'

We went out to face opponents exuding an assured air. They were smugly confident. They had given us the run around in the first half and they had no doubt they would do it again. That, more than George's hype, did the trick. That really fired us up.

From the whistle we hurled ourselves at them, closed them down, knocked them down, and although we gave away too many free kicks we started to win more possession of the ball. They did not like the hard tackling. They hated our sliding tackles which took their legs from under them. Some juicy French curses were thrown our way. But, we got hold of that ball. It was flung out to our two fast wingers. They sped past French defenders trying to turn and fed Aubrey and Mick with beautifully weighted passes and Aubrey came into his own. He became inspired. He turned and twisted and feinted and pulled defenders this way and that and we began to give their goalkeeper some real work. Ten minutes into the second half he slid a diagonal pass behind a French half-back. I ran onto it, slipped a wild tackle and went for goal. The goalkeeper came out. I flicked the ball past, ran onto it and hit it into an empty net. Mick scored a second after a goalmouth mêlée. Aubrey scored a third after a mazy crossfield dribble and a shot low into the corner of the goal. After that, they deflated. We besieged their goal. There was a storm of booing when their goalkeeper was knocked out after a hectic goalmouth scramble. Then, it was all over. We had won by three goals to two.

There was no holding the ebullient triumphant George. He showered his team with praise. Of course, he knew that we would do it. He had never had any doubts about that. Tonight, he proclaimed, we could all go out on the town and he did not give a damn what we got up to.

But it was not to be. Chai had been involved in making arrangements that not even George knew about. Instead of taking us back to the hotel the coach drove us to the Town Hall where we were the honoured guests at a banquet. Maurice Thorez was there, and he made a welcome speech in good English. Chai replied in fluent French. Others made speeches. Toasts were drunk. Aubrey grabbed my shoulder and hissed, 'Hey. Go easy on the wine.' Then he looked at me blearily and said, 'Oh, what the hell. There's always got to be a first time.'

The two teams sat intermingled and I learned a great truth. The French pronunciation I had learned at school bore no relation to the way the French spoke it. Conviviality ruled. After two, three or four glasses of wine I did not know or care what was happening. Bacchanalia ruled and through it all George reddened and beamed and when he was hauled to his feet to make a speech and started off by saying 'I don't know what to say . . .' his team rose to the occasion by chanting in unison, 'You've all got to be in bed by 10 p.m. tonight.'

Our paroxysms of drunken laughter infected our French opponents and they, too, started to fall about helplessly with mirth. Later, outside, another match against Ivry took place. The many steps outside the Town Hall were wide. They were also snowbound. A Frenchman lay down parallel to the top step. Two of his team mates shouted out 'Un. Deux. Trois' and then gave him an almighty push. He rolled over and over

185

down 12 steps before halting. Jock Cohen lay down next. Aubrey and Julius shoved Jock. He only made nine steps down, so the French were leading by one goal to nil. I vaguely remember being grabbed and pushed down onto the snow on the top step and being given an almighty push. Snow got down my shirt collar and melted and I felt uncomfortably wet all that evening. There were embraces and handshakes all round and I remember being thrown into the coach. When we reached the hotel I was roused from sleep and thrown out of it.

We did not enter the Hotel Roblin. We invaded it. The hotel manager and his staff, learning of our win, greeted us with murmurations of 'Felicitations, M'sieurs . . .'. They expressed sadness that tomorrow we would be gone. I saw Chai listening intently to the receptionist. He was smiling broadly and nodding agreement to whatever she was saying. When asked what it was that she was saying Chai said, 'She thinks you are such a grand bunch of boys, very polite, very happy and very amusing. But, when you return next year, could you leave that bad tempered monster, M'sieur le George, behind in England.'

Which is how George acquired his nickname of M'sieur the monster. It was agreed that another game be played next year but the war put paid to that. When we arrived back at Victoria station late on the Monday evening Aubrey and Mick bundled me into a taxi with all the baggage and gave me money for the fare home. Dad was there.

'Well,' he asked, 'did you play on the Sabbath?'

'No, Dad. On the Sunday.'

'Were you careful not to eat *trefa* food?'

'Oh, yes. Eggs, vegetables, bread, you know . . .'

'Did you do your schoolwork?'

I had forgotten to look at it. Mary saw my hesitation and saved the day. 'Please, Mr Beckman, ask him if they won. Did you?'

'We did,' I said gratefully, 'by three goals to two. And Mick, Aubrey and I scored a goal each.'

'Well,' enthused Mary, eyeing Dad, 'isn't that well done . . .'

Dad would never cross Mary. He nodded and said, 'Very good. Now, unpack, have something to eat and go upstairs and do your homework.'

As I was taking my bags up the stairs Mary tapped my shoulder and whispered, 'There has to be one man in the family who doesn't like football.'

Chapter Fifteen

All of a sudden the hundreds of Jewish families in Hackney were grown up and going their various ways, like icebergs splitting away from host glaciers. There was joy and heartbreak, pride and an irrecoverable sense of loss. It happened to us.

Rose married Harry Levy. He was a tailor and owned a menswear shop in the Walworth Road. He was a sunshine character who never took anything too seriously and his favourite saying to anyone down in the dumps was 'There's always someone worse off than yourself'. When he breezed into the house he was always cheery and boisterous. Dad, at first, did not take to him. But Rose and Harry were deeply in love and that transcended everything. He was always sartorially immaculate, with an impeccable sense of matching colour. He sported a toothbrush moustache and liked to wear the white-uppered dancing shoes so popular then.

He was a superb salesman, an impetuous businessman but no deep thinker. An inveterate optimist, his swans invariably turned into geese. Many well-known boxers and wrestlers were his customers and he could always get tickets for any sporting event, even cup finals.

He and Rose bought a house in The Vale, Golders Green, and within a few years produced two daughters, Shirley and Audrey. Part of Harry's business comprised taking his wares onto ships berthing in the London docks. After the crew had been paid off they gravitated towards his temporary shop on the main deck and bought his wares. Once he took me onto a large passenger-cargo boat that was just in. While Harry and his assistant dealt with customers I wandered everywhere. I struck up a chat with a cadet and I asked him where they had been. He replied matter of factly,

'We went down to the Plate and spent ten days in Buenos Aires and Montevideo. Then we went up to Pernambuco in Brazil. It was better than the last trip when we did Freetown and Cape Town.' As soon as I reached home I rushed for the atlas and looked up those glamorous sounding places. Looking back, I know that that short chat changed the direction of my life.

Mary had acquired a regular boy friend, Jim, a fresh faced tousle-haired young builder who worked in his father's firm. Mary had off all day Sunday, a weekday afternoon and, if she wanted it, a few hours here and there. Jim would knock politely at the door and ask for Mary. We would ask him to come in and wait. He would decline. He was very shy and preferred to walk to and fro between our house and the Mitford Tavern until Mary emerged.

Because of Jim we suddenly realised what an attractive woman Mary was. She had a curvaceous figure, long legs and an athletic upright posture. With high cheek bones, full generous lips and auburn hair framing a lively oval face she was, as Mum loyally put it, a film star. When Aubrey asked her where she had been hiding herself all these years she playfully punched him in the chest.

The late summer of 1939 Mary and Jim became engaged. Then, she brought him into the house and made him tea and sandwiches in the kitchen and we would all make ourselves scarce. They married early in 1940 and bought a small terraced house in Edmonton. Mary kept in touch with Mum quite regularly until Jim was called up for the army in spring 1941, then her visits became fewer and fewer and by mid-war stopped altogether. For over 18 years Mary had been a respected and loved member of our family. She averred that she had been lucky to have found us. Without doubt, it was our good fortune that she had.

Freda followed Rose into marriage. Her husband was Hyman Appleton. He was some ten years older than Freda. He was as introverted and as withdrawn as Harry was the opposite. He ran a lucrative pin table, fruit and wall machine business covering over 400 sites in cafes, restaurants, clubs and pubs in Greater London and the Home Counties. He was often out late at nights, as were his roundsmen, repairing machines that had broken down.

During the dark early hours of the morning he was speeding home down a narrow winding Hertfordshire lane when he hit a cow that had wandered out through an open gate. Cow and car were both write-offs. Hyman was damaged, but lucky. After seven weeks he was back at work. He was a workaholic. He built up a substantial property company and was generous towards anyone needing a hand-out.

Aubrey was seldom at home. His firm was sending him to different towns and cities on audits. Mick had left the family business and had started up on his own. He moved from Amhurst Road to a flat off Baker Street. A girlfriend of mine named Doreen sang in a band. The band went on a long tour and Doreen with it. I was desolate. Max, in his inimicable fashion, observed, 'It's amazing what lengths girls will go to to get away from you.'

There was always the on-going nuisance of the fascists. In the late 1930s they basked in the reflected glory of Nazi annexations and General Franco's victories in Spain and their confident arrogance made it dangerous for any unwary Jewish person to be in the wrong place at the wrong time. Although it was a comfort the way the moderate British electorate rejected both fascist and communist candidates in elections they continued to make life intolerable in areas where they held their meetings and rallies. One evening Old Man Clarfelt, a tall and powerful man who had developed strength through having hauled meat carcasses about in his kosher meat business in his youth, looked out through his window and saw his son George being set upon by three blackshirts. He rushed out and plunged headlong into the mêlée. He punched one blackshirt to the ground. The others ran off. One ran across the road and was knocked down by a passing car. An ambulance took him to hospital. No further action was taken by the police who had taken statements.

The attitude of some police at the fascist meetings was disturbing. Of course, they were obeying orders and protecting the tradition of free speech. This was right. But there had to be limits to the obscenity of the verbal provocation that we heard. So we thought. But we were often wrong. Certain police were undoubtedly infected by the toxic virus of anti-Semitism and became known for their unnecessarily brutal reactions against hecklers. Colonel Basil Henriques, a magistrate and the chairman of the East London Juvenile courts, disbelieved police bias until he attended a fascist meeting and saw with his own eyes police standing idly by and watching savage blackshirt attacks on elderly Jews.

On 9 November 1938 an event in Germany scattered even the self-deluding complacency of those upwardly-mobile achieving Jews whose success made them feel totally secure. In a countrywide program, dubbed *Kristallnacht* because so much glass from attacked Jewish properties carpeted the streets, 267 synagogues were burnt and destroyed, more than 1,000 shops were ransacked, over 30,000 Jews were arrested and a collective fine of one billions marks was imposed on the Jewish community. The whole world condemned this paranoic outrage. Unfortunately, condemnations alone can never help the victims of such fury.

Dad could not bring himself to read the newspapers. An unusually subdued Mr Cohen actually left his wireless alone.

The evening after *Kristallnacht* another solemn gathering took place in our house. There were Mr Cohen and Mr Kramer, Mr Galinsky and four other men. Mum and Mary ran the inevitable coffee and cakes shuttle. The men discussed one theme; what could they do to help their German co-religionists. The answer was . . . nothing. They all knew this before they discussed it. But by the discussion alone they felt they were showing solidarity with their less fortunate German brethren.

Inevitably, the conversation turned to a more worrying tack. Could it happen in England? Would they be forced to move again in their lives? If so, where could they run to next? Arguably, the most cheerful Jew in Hackney that week was Issy, when he said '*Habonim* has had a surge of new members. If *Kristallnacht* doesn't make everyone see the right way ahead something worse will come along. You'll see'.

Kristallnacht did stir the pot. Jewish National Fund boxes had never been so heavy with coin and it was more silver than copper. The usual, filleted, keep-your-heads-down rabbinical sermons gave way to uncompromising condemnations of the authorities for letting the fascists get away with open racial incitement. More young idealists of both sexes burnt their boats and made their way to Palestine to work on the land bought by the Jewish Agency. In the East End more young Jews, weary of being passive for so long, turned against the injunctions of the Board of Deputies to keep their heads down and they became more actively militant. Vigilante groups appeared and roaming gangs of blackshirts no longer had the free run of the streets after dark.

Every Friday Dad brought back refugee families and solitaries for a Friday night meal with us. With Freda and Rose gone it did impose a strain on Mum and Mary. Aubrey and I helped out with the to-ing and fro-ing of plates and dishes and even with the wiping up. Occasionally a woman guest would offer to help. Our protestations were never quite strong enough to stop them from helping.

The German refugees were very mixed in their feelings and outlook. There were those who were too Teutonic to be liked. They were convinced that Germany would recover from a temporary madness, then they could return there. A few irritated us by comparing what they had left behind to what they had found in Hackney, to Hackney's detriment. Most were grateful. Later, we received letters and postcards from them post-marked America, Canada, South America and South Africa. Without exception none could credit that England was not re-arming flat out. As a dental surgeon from Leipzig put it

> Hitler is creating a massive war machine. It is an exciting toy. One day he will use it to see what it will achieve. He is a psychopath who has been given total control of a mighty industrialised country and he is a psychopath without any restraint.

Before 1938 ended I left school. It was a wilful decision on my part. I remember the housemaster earnestly urging me to think again. But there were too many reasons against my changing my mind. I had no great desire to go to university. I was one of the majority who had no aptitude to make me want to qualify in this or that profession. I kept diaries. I liked writing and sent off stories to diverse magazines and newspapers. Without success. I was the odd ball in my family. No on seemed to be politically interested and aware of momentous happenings that would affect me more than the passing or failing an examination. Max was very like-minded. We went out a lot together. Older than me, Max passed his Higher Schools with a distinction in mathematics. Yet, with the certainty of war ahead he only wanted to fly. He itched to join the Royal Air Force and he became as quietly obsessed about flying as was Issy with his Zionism.

Aubrey qualified as a chartered accountant. Phil Cohen

became a doctor. Jack Clarfelt qualified as a solicitor. These successes were repeated by the dozen throughout the Hackney Jewish community. The struggles of immigrant parents to support their sons through long years of education were now paying off. Amhurst Road had its full share of triumphs and produced achievers in various spheres of the arts, especially, musicians. Meanwhile, I took a job with the Mentmore and Platignum fountain pen and pencil company in Well Street. I was in the stock control department, checking sales and purchase invoices and keeping index cards up to date. It was tedious, yet I was able to give Mum three pounds ten shillings a week. This made me feel good as well as grown up. But, Dad discomforted me. He made me feel that I was wasting myself in a dead end job. Whereas at school it was my teachers who kept pointing out that I could do better, now Dad was doing it.

With all this achievement everywhere, the ground was quaking under our feet and the invasion of Poland erupted into that climactic morning of 3 September 1939 when Chamberlain announced in that sepulchral voice that Britain was now at war with Germany. I was there with Dad, Mary, Rose, Harry, Mr Cohen, Phil and Bessie. Mr Rapaport came in. So did three or four others. Mum stayed upstairs in her bedroom. She did not want to hear the announcement. After Chamberlain had stopped speaking there was a long sombre silence. No one moved a muscle. Then, suddenly Mr Cohen jumped to his feet. He raised his two clenched fists on high and roared, 'At last. At last, Yossele, we can get after those wicked mamserim [bastards].'

Well, we could, and we did. But not even Mr Cohen could have envisaged at what cost. The extent and depth of the evil that we had to destroy was then beyond imagination. Four weeks later an eager bustling Max came round for me. He said,

'Come on. We're going to Kingsway.'

'What for?'

'To join the Royal Air Force. Just think, we'll learn to fly.'

We walked there and tagged onto a short queue and eventually reached the desk. Behind it sat a lugubrious corporal. He asked disinterestedly what we wanted.

'We want to fly,' said Max enthusiastically.

'You do?' He looked at us disdainfully. 'Don't waste my time. Go back to school.'

Max bristled. 'Don't you know there is a war on?'

'Piss off.' The corporal waved us away. 'It takes brains to fly a plane.'

Max fell ominously quiet. He rested his two hands on the desk and said very politely, 'I do so agree. That must explain why a moron like you is behind that desk.'

We hurried out into the street with Max muttering how Hitler had it made if there were stupid buggers like that in uniform. Over tea and buttered toast in the Tottenham Court Road Lyons corner house, which I paid for as I was earning and this made me feel very mature, I wondered whether Max had told his parents that he intended to fly. He said he would tell them after he had signed up, otherwise he would be engaged in a running emotional battle. I suggested that we try the army, or the navy. Max was adamant. It was flying. Nothing else would do.

The beginning of the war saw the newspapers filling up with advertisements as the country cranked itself onto a war footing. I spotted a quarter pager in *The Daily Telegraph*. It was an Admiralty notice announcing that a continuous radio watch was needed for all British ships at sea and radio officers were urgently required. A crash course of six months was offered, at the end of which applicants who passed the required tests would get a Special Certificate which would qualify them for sea service. It appealed to me. That chat I had had with that cadet on that ship in London docks had never left my mind. I decided to go for that advertisement. I told Max. He tried hard to talk me out of it, to wait and then we could fly together. But suddenly, I was as set on going to sea as he was about flying.

I applied for the course, was accepted and as a result found myself cycling to a marine communications college in Clapham five days a week. I gave up my job and had the unpleasant task of telling Mum that I could not contribute any more to the weekly budget. She just said, 'Don't worry'.

The college was a multi-roomed double-fronted house which had been converted for the required purpose. There were about 50 of us taking the course at that college. They came from every walk of life and from all over the United Kingdom. Most revealed that they had always had a hankering to see foreign parts but never thought they would get the chance. Our instructors had all been marine radio officers.

We took the course very seriously. We were all busting to get away to sea and failure was unthinkable. Accent was on our learning to transmit the morse code and to receive it at faster and faster speeds. The instructors even induced variations of static, while we were receiving, to attune us to problems they said we would encounter. We learned how to dismantle and repair marine transmitters and receivers. They were sturdy machines and not too complicated. We learned the international code and other tasks allied to the job and our instructors were very hot on battery and equipment maintenance.

Close to the college was a cafe owned by an elderly widow who regarded us as her boys. The cafe was named Fanny's. We never knew her surname so we dubbed her Fanny Bagwash. She was an outgoing character with large expressive eyes, hennaed hair and carelessly rouged cheeks. She had an assistant-cum-cook named Dolly who was so fat her pulpy flesh quivered as she moved about. From one to two o'clock those of us who did not bring sandwiches crowded into Fanny's to eat her home-made steak pies and fruity crumbles. These were hilarious rowdy sessions but we all enjoyed the badinage and repartee.

Fanny regarded us as her family. All students who passed the final tests paid Fanny a last visit. Fanny would cook them a final slap-up meal and not charge them for it. Then, she would line up the new radio officers, embrace and kiss them and demand postcards from the ports they reached. Her walls were papered with postcards from all parts of the world and it was fascinating to see how many ports Fanny's boys had reached.

So anxious were the Admiralty to put continuous radio watch on all British ships at sea that we could feel ourselves being pushed hard by our instructors. Every second month there were the final tests and a new batch of radio officers would pass out. My final month there I took the final test along with 11 others. One failed. He was told to stay on and take the tests again. He was so devastated that we persuaded him to come along to Fanny's to enjoy the fun. Nevertheless, it must have been excruciating for him, especially when Fanny lined up those of us who had passed for the kiss and embrace farewell. Fanny had a heart. After she finished with us she went over and kissed the forlorn failure and said, 'Don't be in a hurry to go to war. It's no joke.'

Later, when I read the monthly radio officers' magazine *The Signal*, I saw the casualty lists and came across the names of students who had been with me at college, I understood Fanny's sadness. For a couple of years I did send her postcards from various places and promised, as we all did, that we would visit her. I never did. So many things one determines to do and never gets around to doing.

The college was a stone's throw from where Aunt Golda lived. My second week there, I cycled along to see her. She was surprised and delighted to see me. I told her what I was doing. She listened, open-mouthed, then said, 'Does your father know?'

'No. Mum does. But she's keeping it quiet.'

'I'll bet she's not happy about it.'

'No. She isn't.'

Aunt Golda was ever practical. 'What?' she asked, 'are you doing about food?'

I told her about Fanny's. She threw up her hands and exclaimed, 'I'll bet your father would be mad if he knew what you are eating . . . it can't be kosher.'

'It isn't.'

'Well,' said Aunt Golda, 'you can eat here every day and I'll see you get a nice lunch.' We argued about it, then compromised. I enjoyed lunch at Fanny's so I ate there three times and at Aunt Golda's twice a week.

Max, meanwhile, had made more attempts to join the RAF. They were unsuccessful but, as he said, it was just a question of time. He still grumbled about my going to sea. Mick had got into the RAF and told me he would be flying in a few months. Aubrey was never home. There was a very subdued end-of-an-era feel about Amhurst Road.

After the farewell party at Fanny's I went to see Aunt Golda. We had tea and her strudel and we talked about many things, then she asked,

'When will you go to sea?'

'Quickly. They're rushing us onto ships which need additional radio officers as soon as they dock. I know chaps passing out one day and being on their way to ports all over the country the next day.'

'In that case', said Aunt Golda, 'you must tell your parents the truth today. If you don't I will.' She embraced and kissed me. She was tearful.

'I'll write to you, wherever I land up.'

'No.' She dabbed her eyes and apologised for being foolish. 'Don't write from anywhere. When you get home from a voyage, just phone me.'

31 November 1988. Aunt Golda died in the Nightingale Home For Aged Jews. She was 98 years old. She never had an easy life. Death

had deprived her of two fine husbands and a son. Yet, hardship and tragedy had never kept her down for long. She was buried on 1 December 1988 at Bushey cemetery on a wet chill-wind day. I was the first to shovel earth onto her coffin, after it was lowered into the grave. I was the last to leave her. Freda, the only other member of our Hackney family still alive, kept calling out petulantly with all the lack of inhibition of a widow nearing her eighties, 'Come on. What are you hanging about for? I'm freezing. I'll catch pneumonia.' When I joined her I did not tell her that I was tearful and wanted to compose myself.

I received my Special Certificate and went along to the Marconi International Marine Company in East Ham High Street, where I spent a whole morning filling out forms. The clerk gave me an allowance of £25 and informed me this was an advance which would be deducted from future earnings. He gave me a list of the sea-going gear I should buy and urged me to do it quickly.

That same afternoon I went to Gardiner's, a triangular three-storeyed outfitters specialising in every item required by men going to sea. Its customers were navy and merchant seamen. It was situated on an island site near the docks where Aldgate met Whitechapel and Commerical Road. The site was called Gardiner's Corner, after the shop, which must have coined it during the decades of Britain's maritime might. It was an old building with wooden floors that sagged and rose so unevenly that you had to keep looking down as you walked past the laden shelves. Some of these shelves were beautifully carved and were probably industrial antiques even then. Gardiner's was gutted by fire some 20 years after the war.

I wandered to and fro, up and down, and eventually cleared the list. It was a busy place. The prize purchases were the uniform, with its brass buttons and single wavy gold stripe, the cap and the greatcoat. I bought a voluminous suit-case, packed all the gear into it and caught a number 42 bus back to Pembury Corner, where I jumped out and walked slowly down Amhurst Road. When I banged at the lower street door Sam opened it. He said, 'What the hell have you got in that case?'

'My sea-going gear.'

'Your what?' I repeated what I had said. 'Christ! We sometimes wondered what you were up to . . . You must tell Dad.'

He shunted me into the comforting green gloom of the dining room. I sat down at the table, trembling with apprehension. Sam returned with Dad. Mary was behind them, looking anxious. She sensed drama and stayed by the open door. Dad and Sam sat down at the table. I told them the truth, omitting my dinners with Aunt Golda. No one interrupted me. I stared at Dad. He took off his thin-rimmed circular spectacles and rubbed his eyes. We waited for an explosion of wrath, of disappointment. It never happened. Instead, he turned to the others and said quietly, 'Leave us alone, please. I want to speak to Morris alone.'

When they had gone he looked at me and said quietly, without a hint of reproach, 'Why did you do it? You're too young. And what about your future career? All right, you're not cut out for a profession. You don't particularly want to go to university. What will you do after the war?'

'Dad. I can't think of that until the Nazis are beaten,' I said. 'Look at the refugees we had at this table. Many were at the top of their professions and owned large businesses. Now, look at them, glad to have escaped with their lives. If the German Nazis get here and the British fascists get into power the Jewish solicitor and business tycoon will stand side by side at the execution block with the Jewish cobbler and taxi driver . . .'

We spoke for about half an hour, as equals. On many matters we were not far apart. To my relief Dad never once introduced the topic of Judaism and Jewish traditions. He agreed that fascism in power equated with the destruction of Jewish communities under their power. He was worried about the

200

future, not for himself, but for his family. Then, when he stood up to end the discussion he did something which he had never done before. He came round the table and embraced me with both arms. I reciprocated and at that moment I would have killed any blackshirt who came in to harm him, or Mum. Everything was changing, even the chemistry inside me.

The next day I received a telegram. It told me to report to the *SS Venetia*, a tanker, within 24 hours. She was lying at anchor in the Thames, off Stanley-le-Hope.

'So you're going, then. You're really going.' Mary hugged me and gave me a resounding kiss on my cheek. 'I'll make you your favourite anchovy and tomato sandwiches to take with you.' She did. She made far too many. She must have used up an entire loaf of rye bread. I ate them all.

I phoned Max with the news. He listened without interruption and then he uttered a deep groan. 'Oh, why didn't you wait. The RAF have taken me. I'll be pilot training in no time and we could have done it together . . .' A long silence, and then, 'Oh you silly impatient sod.'

Within one year of that phone call Sergeant-pilot Maxwell Addess took off in his Beaufighter from an airfield in East Anglia. His squadron attacked a swarm of German aircraft over the sea. Max was killed in action.